RINGER OF DUSTY PLAINS

by

John W Barry

RINGER OF DUSTY PLAINS

Author: John W Barry

National Library of Australia Cataloguing-in-Publication entry

Creator: Barry, John Wayne, author.

Title: Ringer of dusty plains / John Barry.

 ISBN: 9780994434302 (paperback)

Subjects: Barry, John Wayne.

Livestock workers--Australia, Central--Biography

Drovers--Australia, Central--Biography.

Cattle trade--Australia--History.

Nineteen seventies.

Dewey Number: 636.213092

Published with the assistance of www.loveofbooks.com.au

ACKNOWLEDGEMENTS

It was early in the 1970's when I rode the Jundah Plains, a small town but a vast countryside.

I worked the Caplin Station, a large cattle station, heading towards Longreach. The mob in the yards were a wild bunch but reliable, they would always have your back. There was Noat, a name given to him whilst sharpening axes years ago, consequently a job not to be undertaken when drunk leaving him with no toes on his left foot. Then there was Terry, the Romanian with attitude (Huh! Imagine that!) As well as the Taylor brothers, Dave and Jack.

CONTENTS

CHAPTER ONE

I will take you back to a night in July when the native animals were on the prowl, the yards were closed and the steeds were fed. One of our thoroughbreds had foaled two days before little Bailey Jo, the colt was a remarkable boy already looking for mischief, but a bundle of laughs to watch. At about ten o'clock heads were down, all was quiet as the lights went out.

The screams of livestock filled the air as a pack of wild dogs made their way into the enclosures and began attacking our animals. By the time we reached for the guns and headed out the back door our steeds had broken out into the darkness of night.

I went looking for Bailey Jo and I felt as empty as the stable that showed signs of ravaged struggle, the ground bruised from where the foal was fiercely lugged away by his attackers. The name Bailey Jo pronounced "bay-lee-jo" was a name of a woman who was kidnapped in the dark of the night and her body found ten days later stoned to death. Her cold, dead body lay beside a place not far from here called Stone Henge, an ancestral burial site. The sacrifice was performed because of her disobeying traditional aboriginal legends. Her ghost is still present after hundreds of years. Some even witness seeing her, others have only felt her presence.

The flashlight cast a vision of twisted branches and overturned stone where the foal had been lugged away. We followed the trail to a ridge, a short walk away where signs of a struggle between Bailey Jo and the hungry canines seem to have taken place with no colt to be seen.

It was breaking light when we headed back to the stables. When we arrived, we were greeted by some of the horses that had made their way back after the canine ordeal.

The morning was spent counting the loss of the yard animals. Ten chickens, two calves and our pet dog Ringo all perished that night in a random attack of fierce and brutal rage. These areas are known for their dog packs.

These vicious canine packs were mostly household pets that have been dumped in the bush to fend for themselves because the bloody useless owners could not be bothered looking after them. It makes me wild! We hadn't had a single attack on our animals and it happened so quickly. All the town folk are quick to blame the dingoes, but that is not true.

It was a late start to the day, the horses were saddled and we took off to check the perimeter fences for any holes or damage where the mongrels could get in. The homestead consisted of a mud brick house which was constructed in the early nineteen hundreds. The yards were scattered across a fifteen hundred acre spread of paddocks and bushland. Down by Ransom Ridge area there are a couple of old shanties. These are small buildings the stockmen used to shelter over the harsh years around the turn of the century. One of them in particular always caught my eye. It was called Maddison Cottage, the only one with a chimney.

I unloaded myself from the steed and shook off the dust as I headed towards Maddison Cottage. A scuttering sound from within made me pause for a moment. With the ordeal that occurred last night still playing on my nerves I thought about retrieving my Winchester from the horse but I decided to go on without it.

Moving forward onto the step, I entered the cottage pushing open the front door. As I checked my surroundings, I found myself looking down the pointy end of a double barrel shotgun.

I looked along the glistening barrel into the eyes of a stranger.

These eyes were somehow familiar but still had a strangeness to them. It took a few moments for me to realise that it was Casper Norton! I had seen an alert on the television a couple of weeks earlier about a fugitive wanted for a home invasion in Blackall. He has been accused of executing a family after holding them hostage for several hours then killing them off, one at a time. It was a gruesome tragedy. He then imprisoned the local copper and the staff at the Blackall Police Station before setting it alight showing no mercy for their screams. I should not have doubted my instincts and brought my gun, but this could be the only way my life is spared.

Quick thinking caused my mouth to move.

I casually said, "G'day! I didn't know anyone was home."

I took a deep breath as I heard the gun cock and click, ready to fire.

"My name is Joseph, a name I don't usually use, so just call me Jo."

Around town, we have a code. If you're ever faced in such a situation, you use your full name and anyone close by would know that you need help. Except that Romanian Terry, we'd leave that asshole to fend for himself! I stood there silently thinking stupid thoughts like 'shit, I'm hungry, I forgot brekky today' but all I wanted was my last meal before I died.

My gut started growling. Casper grinned and said, "Who else is with ya?"

I didn't reply. The law of the land was if you point a gun, then use it. So far he hadn't so I had him bluffed. Holding the shotgun to my head as he waited for my reply, the Taylor boys had got wind of my predicament. Dave, a rather big lad of solid build, and Jack, a skinny lanky useless piece of shit, stood outside calling my name.

"Jo," then a slight pause, "Jo, are you there?"

He yelled out loud not knowing that I was just a couple of feet away inside the cottage. Jack had made his way to the roof. Luckily, these old shanties had a trap door for ventilation. The vent was open. We were in luck! As Jack lowered a noose that he made for chasing stray cattle, the shank loose and wide, I didn't even bothered looking up. Jack did what Jack did best. With a flick of the wrist, he'd captured Casper around the neck. This was my only opportunity to drop to the floor. As my body hit the floor, the first shot fired, ringing in my ear. The second shot hit my foot with full blast. I fell out and down the step falling into a painful heap.

Dragging my leg along, I watched Casper reload. Dave had joined Jack on the roof and with one hefty heave they lifted Casper off the floor. The shotty pointed towards the ceiling I knew I had little time. The ground beside me was covered in old kitchen tools so I reached out for the iron and in one fowl swoop I sent it toward Casper's head. The Taylor boys, seconds from death, rope in hand, jumped from the roof. The shotgun blast echoing across the plains. All was quiet as I slowly moved to a crack in the boards where these walls had dried during the drought. I jumped as the gun hit the floor. I could see that murdering swine strung up like a wild boar that had been culled.

My foot shattered and torn, my aboriginal brothers stood with big wide grins.

"WE GOT HIM, WE GOT HIM" They chanted.

We soon came to the realisation that we had committed the taking of a life. We tried to work out what to do. Jack was on probation, Dave had issues of his own, and the local copper hated my guts after the affair his mother and I had about five years ago. Our only solution was to keep this to ourselves.

My foot still pulsating with pain, I attempted to stop the bleeding without much luck. Dave and Jack helped me onto my horse as I lay limp over the saddle.

"Nessy will get you home Jo, she knows the way! Leave everything to us," said Jack. "Don't say a word brother."

After a painful journey back to the homestead, I fell to the soil. Weak and drained I made my way to the stables with just enough energy to roll into the water trough, too exhausted to go any further. When Dave and Jack returned nobody spoke a word. Jack was removing the gear from the horses shaking his head looking at the blood filled trough. I had my leg up in a make shift splint, made by two tent pegs and some electrical tape. Not real flash, but it will do.

A few months later, I was straining the south fences when a silver BMW approached. A tall, attractive woman stepped out. It was Julie Archer. Daughter of the Mayor of Longreach, until two years ago.

Wow! How a few years makes a difference. She was only a teenager when she left five or six years ago.

"G'day Jo, do you remember me? It's Julie."

"Yes," I replied, looking her up and down amazed by her adult transformation.

I made my way through the fence to greet her. We don't go into Longreach much anymore. Making the change to the quiet life meant trips to town were very far and few between. Once a month to gather supplies is about it.

We chatted for a while and I asked how her family were. With a pale, faint look on her face she began to reply in a stuttering voice of the tragedy involving the loss of her family in the siege at Blackall a few months ago. Living a quiet life you hear of things that happen but not to whom. This news shocked me. I asked her to join me for dinner up at the homestead. She accepted. I could see the heartbreak in her eyes. I no longer felt guilty of Casper Norton's demise that day. An eye for an eye, I say.

Arriving back home with Julie following closely behind, I parked the Dodge Ute by the carport, leaving the covered park for Julie's flash car as the Australian outback can be harsh on the paint so the shelter is always open for good cars. Anyway, the old Ute has seen better days.

I opened the door to the homestead and escorted Julie inside. Jack was cooking dinner. As a fantastic aroma of spices filled the air, my guts growled at such an inappropriate moment.

Embarrassed, I yelled to Jack, "We have a guest!"

Jack peered around the kitchen door, dropping to the spoon to the floor and muttering, "Who's the chick?"

"This is Julie. You remember Alex Greystone's cousin?"

Twelve months earlier Jack had stolen Alex's old HQ Holden Ute.

Jack replied sarcastically, "Oh yeah! I recall a pimple-faced, snotty-nosed kid. But surely it's not her?"

"Yep!" Julie said, "You low life, thieving shithead."

I laughed and replied, "now that you two have reminisced, kiss and make up."

As much as I felt compelled to inform Julie of what had happened to Casper Norton, the mongrel who killed her Mum, Dad and two brothers, I just listened as she broke down telling me of how her life has been ripped apart and if she got hold of that scum bag Casper Norton she would string him up!

Both Jack and I looked at each other confused and bewildered.

"Yeah, I hope the bastard hangs," almost simultaneously, Jack said nervously.

"Um yeah," I said, "What Jack said!" Phew!

"What's for dinner Jack?" Dave announced as he walked in the door, stripping off his dirty clothes.

"Bloody had to kill that cat, the crazy thing had its head caught in a rabbit trap! It was a goner, so I put it out of its misery."

Dave being Dave, headed towards the bathroom, passing the dining room where Julie and I sat in only his flannelette shirt and jocks. By the time Julie and I turned around, Dave was standing there with his pride and joy swinging in the breeze. I am not a jealous type, but no one needs seven inches on the slack.

"Cover up!" I bellowed, "We have company."

Julie's head flicked back faster than Jack could rope, holding her hands over her eyes. I chuckled and I could see the grin on her face.

The evening settled down and Dave dressed accordingly. Jack had been making a stew, his own concoction and I treated myself to seconds. I spotted headlights through the trees; the single driving light on the right hand side of the vehicle led me to believe Noat was back. Noat had flown to Alice Springs to see his father in prison. It had been four years since the pair had met but he needed his father's signature for ownership of Caplin Station to be completed.

I walked back to the dining table and Julie noticed my limp. "Hey, that's new."

Puzzled, I stopped, unaware of my leg being in her line of sight.

"The limp in your walk. What happened?"

"What is what?" I replied.

"Your walk. You have a problem with your foot."

I hesitated for a moment, then Noat busted in the door.

"Hey you numb nutter turds, can't a bloke get a hand to bring in his kip?" Noat said with a half-cocked grin and a one finger salute.

"Noat, you dirty dog! You're back!" Jack yelled as he tackled him to the floor knocking down the photos from the wall.

"You bloody idiot Jack!" Dave teased and whacked Jack on the back of the head with a heavy hand.

"Sorry brother," Jack replied with a cautious shuffle out of the way of Dave's big hand.

Attention was set on Noat's return and Julie sat alone at the table not knowing what to do.

"Oh shit!" I blurted out, "Sorry Julie, I forgot all about you sitting there. This is Noat, his father owns the property."

"Not anymore," Noat said "It's mine now, and the beers are on me!"

By two o'clock in the morning Julie was exhausted and slumped on the couch in the corner, snuggled up to her beer. The rest of us left her and headed to bed.

Five a.m. is always starting time around here no matter what time we hit the sack. The four of us headed out searching for Terry the Romanian drover on the plains. About three hours into the ride we arrived at the camp. We located Terry in his usual loveable mood.

Don't scare the herd, you fucking clowns!" He said in that wild, off beat voice. "No time to chin wag, get your asses to work!"

"Hey!" Dave said. "What happened to the girl?"

Looking at each other we shrugged our shoulders. With blank looks on our faces it came to us that Julie was still out cold back at the homestead.

Bringing the herd up to speed, we headed towards the Jundah sale yards. The journey took most of the day. The dry desert heat was blowing in from the west and the sand and wind filled the air with choking results. Water was plenty for us but the cattle were slow and weary.

Turning north along the break there were five brumby's watching us. They fed on the only patch of grass that existed on these baron plains. I drew my whip and with one sharp crack I sent them on their way. You see, the brumbies around here are wild horses. One or two are not bad, but any more than that the take over the grazing areas for the cattle. We have to preserve what little feed there was.

Life was throwing us a sour twist this year and with one more days driving, the trek will finally end and hopefully we should get a good price per head.

The arid land was a sight during the dry season, the massive cracks in the ground can open up to six feet wide the hard section called the break had a stone sort of slate base which always held solid. We headed out of the break into Molly's Ridge, two abreast we rode, keeping the herd inline the ridge stepped up four feet higher. I don't know why, but some sort of fault in the ground due to earthquake thousands of years ago. To be honest, I never thought about it until now.

On top of the ridge we could look back towards the southern sky. A big storm front was rolling in.

"It don't good look!" Noat called out.

Dave spun around knowing Jack has always had the ability to read the sky. There was no doubting that it was time to set up camp for the night, although it was still daylight, it was best for the sake of all.

Meanwhile, back at the homestead, Julie had woken after sleeping all day dazed and puzzled. She staggered around the house not knowing where she was. Firstly checking her purse and checking her car was outside and finally making sure her knickers were still on as she knew her own reputation when she had too much to drink. She was happy to know this was not the case as far as the tell-tale signs showed.

Looking around the house with no one to be seen she slipped out to her car, still puzzled by where and why she was there, her memory of the night before very vague. Climbing into the car and heading out towards the gate, she was still trying to find signs of life. The property was deserted.

Julie headed into town as she drove looking back in the mirror the clouds were shadowing her every mile of the way.

Going back down to the break, our camp only consisted of a few swags and a rock perimeter fire. Terry stayed on the ridge and the cattle were locked in for the night.

Dave set for the first watch, fitted out wearing his jacket that belonged to his old man from the war. Terry never talked much just grunted whilst Jack was busy stirring the shit out of Noat who was attempting to catch Jack. Jack was quicker than a greyhound chasing a feed. Noat hopelessly failed as it was a cat and mouse tale to tell.

A few raindrops started to fall, then out of nowhere it came down quick. By the time we entered our swags, it had rained almost an inch within the first hour. Then a light drizzle set in. Wet and uncomfortable, the best method of trying to rest was to lock yourself in your swag and keep in it until morning. The night seemed to go on forever, going down early in the bad weather always made you feel that way. I woke about four in the morning. Jack was on watch sound asleep as usual. Just a bloody good thing the cows knew to behave. As I gave him a kick in the ribs, he stirred like a field mouse. I would like to know what he was dreaming about, but it's probably a good idea I don't!

"Yo!" I called out attempting to wake the boys.

My comment was met with not very savoury replies. A good crew can get riding in ten minutes like precision clockwork. Terry headed out to the ridge as we drove the cattle through the trail to the rise. Jack followed, as Noat and Dave spread out keeping the herd boxed in. Around two o'clock we saw the sale yards in sight. I don't know if it was the cattle glad to be rid of us or us wanting to have a good meal at the pub that drove us to a more vigorous pace. It was not a flash old pub, but the knockers on Joanne the bar maid had their own postcode they were so huge. A bonza looking sheila but not one to take shit from anyone.

Joel, the sale yard jock, had the gates open and the first head of cattle made their way in. Closing the back yards allowed Terry to follow with the remainder. As always, one steer shot back out as the gate was shut. I saw it break, and Tapper, the new colt, cut in and had a firm grip on the task at hand, so much so, I almost lost my footing. One foot in the stirrup, I was caught by surprise as Tapper had no intention of letting this beast get the upper hand.

Finally seated back on the saddle, I went about adjusting myself. I gave the new horse my seal of approval, stroking his mane and patting his neck. We carried on to the stables to unsaddle the horses for the night and I saw Dave and Jack already on the pub veranda with a couple schooners.

"He a bit quick for ya, Jo?" yelled Noat.

I replied, "Nah, just testing him!"

"Sure," Terry commented.

The night was highlighted by another beautiful Australian sunset with a haze of shimmer in the sky, we enjoyed a big hefty meal and set in for the evening.

CHAPTER TWO

A month had passed since we drove the cattle to town. The dry, dusty plains have grown weary and almost baron. The feed has vanished, the dams are dry, and life has frozen in the dusk of time. All we could do is the maintenance on the property.

Although we made good dollars at the auction, the fences and upkeep of the homestead can be very draining on the finances if we don't keep an eye on the funds. Toby Henderson has about three hundred head of yearlings up for sale and I am trying to talk Noat into purchasing them. We could resell a few and sit on the rest for another six months.

Adam Swartz arrived with his daughters, Jane and Kimberley. A great family that own the local meat works at Jericho. It has been about three years since last they visited. Unfortunately, his wife packed her bags and left the girls with Adam to raise. Jane is only fifteen but the best barrel racer in the state, whilst Kimberley is probably the most mechanical minded person this side of Ilfracombe.

"What do you want?" Terry yelled. "Get off the property or Betty will bite ya!" Betty being Terry's rifle which seems to appear at random, almost from thin air.

"Hang on, you stupid Romanian prick," Adam replied. "I need you to do some work for me."

Noat told Terry to shut up whilst Jack and Dave stood with mouths open drooling over the girls.

"Hands off, you shitheads!" Adam remarked in a way that sent shivers down your spine. Adam stood six foot seven and weighed 190 kilos, with a mean streak a crocodile wished to have.

"I need some trees moved from Tennant Creek to Injune. Do any of you no hopers have a licence?"

"I do," I replied. I had travelled the beef road for quite a few years. I have done a fair bit of road train work for Col Stevens at Durrambandi a few years ago. I thought that if he was to ring up the Stewart's roadhouse they would know about me as Tom was Adam's cousin.

"Good then, you are just who I need."

We discussed the work for a while and decided to take it on. Most of the work was done around here so the thought of something different sounded very cool.

Two days later, Terry, myself, Jack and Dave turned up at the Swartz homestead. It was a privilege just being able to drive on a sealed roadway, a bit of a novelty out here. Adam drove from the rear of the barn to greet us.

"Come on, we will get you started."

Down the fence line, over the rise, the sight of twenty well equipped road trains parked in allocated bays was overwhelming to say the least. Pulling alongside the MACK truck setup with triple trailer combination, we stepped onto the manicured grass.

"Bloody hell!" We all said.

"Should have brought the horses, they could do with a bit of this. You see, there is an artesian bore that runs through this place," Adam said. "We never run out of water." Sigh.

We dropped our shoulders with jealousy.

"Take old Elsie," Adam spoke pointing to the newest truck in the fleet. "She's a new one, only got her last week. The run will break her in."

This truck was well set up for the heat in the outback with an eight foot bunk a lot better than the two foot wide one in the truck I drove years ago. We hopped out and started looking around, smelling the new paint and checking the equipment. Terry took the passenger seat whilst Jack and Dave had room in the bunk to ride. All ready to go, Adam gave us the mud map and told us when and where to meet Tim O'Neil at Tennant Creek. I sat high in the saddle like I was braking in a new steed, perched up on our seats, off we went. It took two days to get to Tennant Creek, which was a bit longer than expected. Pulling up at the Three Ways roadhouse (named for the reason) you could either go to Darwin, Alice Springs or Queensland. Turning around at the pumps, I stopped to fuel up. Climbing down from the long drive our legs were all over the place.

"Got bloody jet lag" Jack laughed!

We could get a beer and a feed inside, generally in that order. I finished fuelling Andersen up heading in to join the others.

"T-Bones are on me!" said Terry.

"I am not having no bloody chop," I replied. "Hey! If it's got a bone, it's a bloody chop! Give me a rump!"

"Buy your own then," Terry said with a not so keen look on his face.

The manager told us Mr O'Neil had set us up in air conditioned cabins for the night.

"No shit" we said. "You're having a go at us, aren't you?"

"Nope, here's the keys."

Wow! One each! We felt like kings for a night at least.

Taking a few cans of beer with us to finish off the night. Well actually, two slabs of beer.

"I had enough," I said.

"You're weak," Jack replied, as he fell over the garden hose heading into the bushes to have a leak.

I don't know what time we all hit the sack but we were out

like a light. No one even stirred. At about five thirty, a lot of machinery noise awoke us. Except Jack, of course! I bet I know who finished the last of the beer. A bit of a wash and California poppy to slicker the hair back, I was set for the day and into the restaurant to have some brekky. I found Dave, Terry and yes, Jack, all slumped over the table. I looked out the window and could just see the front of the truck. I was watching as the cab shook with a solid jolt.

"Some bastard has just run into the rig!" I yelled, pulling the sleeves of my shirt up in preparation for a fight. On exiting the servo we were amazed that the trailers had been filled with massive bottle trees.

"That's it boys!" We heard from a crew of about fifteen blokes. They had been working placing the trees into the tippers or dump truck bodies as the yanks would say.

"Which one of you lot is Jo?"

"That's me," I replied.

"Okay, they're all set, ready to go when you're ready." He held out his hand and said "Tim's the name." He then climbed into his land rover handing me a new mud map of where we had to go. I looked down to check out the paper when almost instantly Tim and the crew took off with no 'see ya later' or nothing!

We headed back inside to have a feed, and with Jack still dead to the world, we woke him up and set him up with rice bubbles. No greasy food for this lad. Last thing we need is chunks in the bunks as they say. The rest of us had bacon and eggs and headed on our way. Before I went out, I stopped and phoned Noat, who was back at the homestead looking after the place. A short call, as we only had a single wire community telephone line. You had to talk fast or old Maureen the telephone operator would listen and put her two bobs worth into the conversation. Everything was okay; I let him know we would be back about next Thursday or Friday when we finish the run.

All ready to go, the morning sky caused a blistering heat. Although the sunrise was well over, the light drove a splendour of enhancement across the desert landscape. It is really a fantastic lifestyle out here. If a tree falls down then it may end up being a location guide to that big hole or dip in the road for the next ten years. Road maintenance is not really good around these parts, crews only come out to patch the road every three months. When we get closer to Longreach, Dave will meet Noat and travel back to help on the property whilst me and the other two kept going to Injune.

It was a day and a half later, we pulled into the Caltex service station to refuel and drop off Dave. Noat was there to meet us as we rolled up. As the MACK come to a stop, out we clambered. Looking a bit worse for wear, Noat shook his head and laughed as Jack slipped and got his shirt caught on the door handle, holding him suspended like a puppet on a string. Dave grabbed his gear and threw it on the back of the Ute.

Terry shouted out. "Hang on, wait for me, I am coming with you!" As he tucked his bag in beside Dave's.

"You don't need me. Besides, another day with that dickhead Jack, I swear I will throttle him!" Terry said looking back at Jack, who was still attached to the handle.

"Well give us a hand to get this joker back in the truck then," I commented.

To which Terry replied, "I'll get the little shit," and with one big jolt he lifted Jack clear off the hook he was hanging from and threw him down on the ground.

Jack, covered in dust and stones, shook himself off and gave a mouth full of cheek. Terry headed at him in a hurried pace quicker than a rabbit, in the cab with the doors locked Jack sat giving Terry the finger.

"I had better go before you tear Jack apart," I said, climbing back into the rig and started the engine to build up air ready to move out.

The next afternoon we arrived at Injune, the gates to the wealthy looking homestead open as we approached looking down a long, wide driveway. We continued until we were stopped by a couple of security personnel. Slowly I came to a halt beside a large excavator ready to plant the trees.

Out of the massive rig we stepped onto the pebbled pathway. Jack and I were escorted from the truck to the homestead. It was massive dwelling like I had never seen before. Into the foyer, a large smorgasbord had been arranged for us all to eat.

Both Jack and I could have stayed there all day feasting on the tucker.

"Well we had better get you back," said a loud solid man. "James Templar's the name. You boys have done a great job, if you have finished I will get you out of here and back to Longreach by dark."

Jack looked at me, puzzled, as we shrugged our shoulders wondering where this clown's magic wand was hidden. A lady came in wearing like a pilot outfit and asked us to follow her to the pad.

"What about the truck?" I said.

"Don't worry about that. I will just give Adam the money for it next time I see him."

I have never heard people talk about a hundred thousand dollars as if it was pocket change. It felt uncomfortable and far from my style of living.

We exited through the rear of the house and there in front of us, sat a big, shiny 12-seater plane.

"What do you think?" The big man said. Jack, crazy as usual, was jumping around hitting his head on the propeller.

"Settle down, you twit!" I yelled as I gulped at the same time as I have never flown in a plane before. I get wonky climbing onto the stable roof. We climbed in and Tim, the owner, handed Jack a lunch box.

"That's your money," he said. "And by the way no one knows of your business trip. There is the eight grand there for the work you have done."

This was equivalent to a year's wages for a strapper. Then he reached out and put some cash into Jack's and my shirt pockets.

"That's for you two for being the only ones to follow through with the job."

"Thanks" I replied as Jack lifted his jaw of the floor of the plane.

Music was playing, it had one of those 8 track tape players unlike the reel to reel one we have back home. 'Leaving on a jet plane' was playing, John Denver was well liked at the bushman's ball, all the locals would try to copy him but no one could get close. All strapped in, Jack distracted me from my fears by singing out of tune to the music, it almost sounded like Chad Morgan choking on a cat.

Up in the air, the smell of a new plane was great but then again anything new smelt good to Jack. I leaned over and grabbed the lunch box the man had given us and upon opening it I saw the cash, and for some reason that I still don't understand, a packet of peanuts.

"Awesome," I said.

"Crikey!" Jack replied. "Look at all that loot."

Within minutes of being in the air, the plane was heading downwards.

"Shit," I said nervously grabbing hold of the seat. "Are we going to crash?"

"No," the lady pilot replied with a reluctant giggle. "We're about to land."

I sighed with relief and locked myself in for the final approach. I had almost forgotten about the cash Tim had put in our pockets. Removing it from my pocket, I revealed a thousand dollars of twenty dollar notes banded together.

"Jack! Jack!"

"What now?!" he muttered, looking my handful of notes. "Holy shit! Where did you get that?"

"It was in my pocket. How much did you get?" Without a second thought, he ripped his pocket open in such a rush and holding his bundle of notes he shouted "I'm rich, I'm rich!" You see, a month's wages for a yard hand was 180 dollars, so to get this much at once was like an inheritance.

Safely, the plane landed but neither of us noticed as we were too excited about our good fortune.

Out we stepped onto the tarmac, still hyped up. We thanked the pilot for the ride and decided we had better try and get a lift into town as old Maureen, the telephonist, has dinner at seven and no phone calls anywhere after that. As we approached the main road, I put my thumb out and just like that, the next car stopped.

"Hello strangers! What are you doing?" It was Julie.

"We need a lift into town," I replied. Longreach airport is close but still a long walk to a phone box.

"Hop in," she said. "I will take you there."

I sat in the front seat whilst Jack climbed in the back. Once we got into town Julie remarked, "I might as well take you out to the homestead."

I replied, "Thanks, but Jack wants to be dropped off near the service station." It had just gone dark.

"I will stay with Macca." Macca was his mate that lived two blocks away from the service station.

It felt like hours when the car began to brake and pull off the road.

"Thanks heaps, Julie," and with that, Jack hopped out of the car at the service station, and headed to over where Macca was standing.

We hit the road again for a while, heading towards Caplin Station when I looked over at Julie, her top two buttons on her blouse had mysteriously come undone to reveal the soft skin of her bust. As I looked down, her skirt was pulled up just enough that I could see her knickers. I tried not to make it obvious that I was looking, but I think that was her idea to attract my attention.

Driving the 200 kilometres to the property takes around three hours. It was a lovely gesture for her to give us a lift. About an hour and half into the trip, I commented on the size of the moon tonight and how it lit up the inside of the car. Julie had undone her bra all the way. It was an amazing view of breasts that moved ever so gently with every bump along the way.

"There is a pull off area for the large cattle trucks ahead," Julie turned to face me and continued. "I need to stretch my legs. It has been a long drive from visiting my uncle in Injune. So where did you and Jack go today Jo?"

"Ah, umm! Just out to Charleville to look at some cattle," not wanting her to know where and what we had been up to as Tim told us to keep it to ourselves.

The car came to a stop and we got out. There was a cool breeze and the moonlight set a fantastic mood. Julie sat on the hood of the car and removed her blouse. "That feels better," she said. I really needed to have a leak so I headed towards the back of the car into a shallow ditch. The relief was soul-gratifying. I walked back to the car with my hands still fondling with my zipper. Julie was laying on the hood of the car absolutely naked. I could not avert my eyes.

"Do you feel better, Jo?" She asked as her ran her hands down her body. Not knowing what to say, I sat beside her. Wow, what a body! Every bump and curve of it had a sensuous glow.

"You are beautiful," I shyly commented as I hid my head away like a love struck teen.

"Come on, silly! Join me. It feels great. Now, take your clothes off before I rip them off!" She was laughing by now and with a slight giggle off went my shirt, then my jeans, leaving my boots and jocks.

"You bloody country boys are all the same. Get your fucking clothes off and get over here, you fool!"

By this time we had become rather aroused. I don't know why but I held my hands across my already rock-hard erection but all that had done was make me more excited. The next ten minutes were spent just lying beside each other, touching hands looking at the blanket of stars being lit up by the full moon. It was excellent. I moved over closer kissing Julie on the lips, slowly caressing her hair, all the time my pulse was racing faster and faster. Her arms raised up and her hand wrapped around me.. We continued until we could not help from locking our hips together, thrusting with a slow, timeless rhythm and moving as the passion of the night sky possessed us into a wild frenzy of sexual love filled delight.

We lay worn out and exhausted with sweat pouring off our glistening bodies. We talked for a while until falling into a deep sleep.

A few hours later, the sound of a truck air horn woke us with a fright. We looked around to see a rig passing by.

"Fuck!" Julie screamed. "That was my bloody cousin Jake, driving that thing!" She grabbed her clothes and jumped into the car to hide, which was really a bit too late as there is no one else anywhere to be seen.

I muttered, "Oh shit."

I tried hard not to grin as being seen with Julie would be awesome, but to be in this predicament overwhelmed me. I was hoping someone else would come along and spot us. Yes, I silently punched my arm into the air, out of sight of Julie.

I glanced down at my watch, seven o'clock. We threw our clothes back on and attempting to look somewhat respectable was no easy task. We decided to get back on the road and headed towards the homestead. I spotted Jake's truck parked out front of the house.

"Oh shit!" We both shouted. Julie brought the shiny BMW to a stop.

"What do we do?" I asked, "If we take off now they will see us."

"I guess we keep on going," Julie suggested, "Here goes nothing!"

The 100 foot long piece of dirt leading up to the property seemed like it went forever. As we moved along hesitantly, we suddenly noticed an ambulance out by the side door. "What's going on here?!" I said anxiously. Before the car had even come to a complete stop, I hit the ground running. I entered the house at a great lot of knots to see Jake on a stretcher, he was out cold.

"What the! What's going on Noat? What happened?"

"He just walked in the door and collapsed for no reason, Jo," he replied.

"Is he alright?"

"I don't know, they have him breathing again, that's all they told us," Dave said as they looked worryingly towards Jake.

The ambulance took off down the long dusty road. On the way to Longreach hospital, Julie had been in touch with her aunty, who advised us that the family were on the way to meet him there.

We later found out that Jake was bitten by a brown snake as he was entering the property. Lucky Dave was there, or he would've been a goner!

Julie and I were standing on the veranda talking when Dave interrupted, "Where the hell is Jack!?"

Without even thinking, I replied "We left him in town last night."

"And you're just getting here now?"

Julie looked puzzled.

"Besides that, why did Jack stay in town?" Dave asked now looking more intrigued than ever.

"I don't know! He was going to Macca's place."

"Hmm, okay. I will go in and pick him up later, I guess," Dave replied.

I spent most of the day with Julie feeding and grooming the horses. Although she came across as a bit of a princess, she never once hesitated to get the tools and trim the horse's hooves. She was quite aggravated by the state the horse's hooves were in and exclaimed, "How can you leave these poor animals so neglected. Grrr!"

With his head down in shame, Dave said, "I'm going to get Jack!" He was just clearing out of the firing line of Julie's comments.

"Chicken!" I yelled, as he quickly jumped into the Ute and sped down the dusty driveway.

It got late into the afternoon before Dave returned with no Jack in sight. He shook his head, not realising Julie was still here and proceeded to rant and rave.

"Jack never went to Macca's! Honey Willson said she had seen Jack get on a bus last night and nobody knows where he was heading! Just that he went west. If that fucking idiot says anything about that bloody Casper Norton, we're up shit creek!"

"WHAT'S THAT ABOUT CASPER NORTON?!"

A voice screamed out from behind the shed. Julie came rushing around, with eyes burning like a crazy woman.

"If I catch that bastard, I will kill him. WHERE IS HE?!"

"You idiot Dave, now look what you stirred up!"

"Well she doesn't have to worry, he is probably fertiliser and pig food by now. Oh! Don't look at me like that Jo, the bitch should have stayed away. Why did you bring her back?"

With those last words spoken I let fly with a right hook, knocking Dave to the ground. About to go for another shot, Julie said, "Leave him alone! And what the bloody hell is he talking about? Don't give me any bullshit, Jo. I want to know NOW!"

"Well we had no choice."

The story was told and it was a massive relief.

Dave, who was still annoyed at me, jumped in his Ute and took off in a fury of thundering dust.

CHAPTER THREE

Two months had passed without a word from Jack since he somehow disappeared when we dropped him off at Longreach. Honestly, I thought after a couple of days he would have turned back up at the homestead. Dave, Terry and I were trying to keep on top of everything, not realising just how much we had come to depend on Jack.

Julie also was distant since finding out about how we dealt with Casper Norton. This has made Dave highly strung and saying very little, not at all happy with the events leading up to filling Julie in on what happened.

The rain had been a bit scarce over the past weeks and it doesn't take long to gather dusty horizons as the wind blows through. My task for today was to go out to where the cottages were and just check the fences are loaded up with wire and hitching gear. I set off for the long journey. Word in town is a chopper had flown low and noticed brumbies running rampant around the area, so it's very common that fences are damaged when the horses tear through the district.

My shotgun was close in hand as I rounded Ransom Ridge. It can be very cruel out there, especially when the brumbies have a go at the stock horses. I guess it is like a domination of territory. I pulled up beside Maddison Cottage and set my gear down. It was a good idea to explore the perimeter fences before taking the tools of trade up there, as the rugged terrain could be hazardous for horse and workman. I threw myself up on the steed just as the wild horses came pounding through like a mini tornado, stripping the ground of any growth around both sides of the cottages. They flew like a thundering charge of devastation. I reefed the reins and ran with them to avoid being knocked off my horse. I managed to cut loose from the pack but not before I was kicked by a random hoof lashing out. My leg was shattered but the pain was the last thing on my mind as I tried to survive this ravaged game of untamed terror.

The dust settled and the wild steeds cleared, leaving a trail of broken shrubs and twisted wire as they broke the fences on their way through. I headed back to Maddison Cottage to take a good look at my leg. It had gone numb but still painful as hell. I lowered on to the step lifting my leg with my hand, putting my weight on the foot. I collapsed with pain, noticing bone sticking out through the flesh.

I dragged myself inside. The cottage was small but well decked out. The smell of mould filled the air and the taste glued itself to my tongue with every breath. No one had been there since the day we had the run in with Casper.

I used the fencing pliers to cut away my jeans. The blood started to pulsate from my wound, somehow the material had held the pressure but now it was soaked with the flow of blood. Managing to seal the wound with an old piece of leather and my belt, I must have faded in to a deep sleep as the exhaustive drama had me beat.

It was getting on in the evening when I woke to the stampede of horses on their way back through. Ear piercing screams could be heard as my stock horse was attacked and killed in this vicious forty to one fight. Moving to the window to watch, not a thing I could do as my gun was on in the saddle holster. Trampled so bad, the horse was barely recognisable. I had left a large container of water in the cottage when I first arrived, which was the only good luck to be granted today.

Unable to stand, I dragged myself to the door swinging it open to clear the dust that had been created inside during the fight outside. I became weary as the sun was going down and in another hour it would be dark. Looking around, I could see some candles, a kerosene lamp and some kero. This would have been fantastic, except I don't smoke and had no way to light anything. Lying there with not much I could do, I saw a horse on the ridge.

"Oh no! Shit!" I yelled. Those bloody brumbies are coming back to finish me off. Good horses, but like anything else, if you get too many together, it is a recipe for disaster. Looking at this one horse, I realised it was alone and glaring into my eyes. It started making its way down the ridge, frantically charging toward the open door. I froze and could not move to get the door shut in time. Barrelling down, the steed stopped about thirty feet away and the markings caught my attention. It was Bailey Jo!

"Bailey Jo? Boy, is that you?"

An alarmed and a fearsome look of kill flashed in his eyes. Raring up high and shuddering back to the earth. My heart stopped. I was in his sight. I was a goner. Moving towards me, he held himself low. The horse, although breathing hard and trembling, he came closer to nudge my face with his nose. It wasn't pleasant, but a damn lot better than being stomped on.

It was like he was a foal again, rolling around in the dust and making noises that were like a beautiful song in my ears. My boy was alive.

With the pain of my broken leg making me weary, I found it hard to move. Thinking of how to get help was something not so easy to do in the outback. It was then that I noticed Bailey Jo lower his ass to the ground, followed by his front legs. He laid down with his stomach on the ground. He was beautiful. In the fading light, the big boy looked like a sphinx. The fore legs badly scarred and his wither distorted from what looked like injuries sustained from his attackers the last time I saw him. The horse sat looking calm and relaxed. I dragged myself

29

towards him, holding his mane to get closer. It was a foolish idea but I tried to pull myself up onto his back. His ears alert and his eyes drawn back he was wild looking and very worried. Totally out of my comfort zone, I eventually got onto this wild, unbroken steed holding his mane. Bailey Jo raised his solid quarters to a full stance, raring slightly. Not knowing how to react, he settled down and the both of us stood still and waited to know what will happen next.

The blood was flowing freely from my leg now, sitting upright has fed the wound with a gush of enormous pain, which felt a lot like my skin tearing apart. I undone my belt and tightened it onto the bone entrusting out of my flesh. Applying pressure, I controlled the loss. Up on the back of this horse of solid appearance, I felt uncomfortable almost to the point of trying to ride a 44 gallon drum down a river. I moved my butt towards the rear and put my head on the wither. Holding the mane firmly, the horse moved in a forward motion. Unsteadily, we started to trek away from the cabins. I had no way of altering where the horse would wander, but hoping I would be found closer in towards the homestead if I fell off.

Almost two hours later and it was pitch black. My line of sight had vanished when the sun went down. I had not a clue of where we were heading. My eyes adjusted to the dark and I noticed the water tank from behind the homestead and I knew we had arrived.

It was all dark inside the house. I yelled out but Bailey Jo panicked with my call and I fell hard onto the dirt snapping my leg in two. Off into the darkness of night he bolted out of sight. Fuck! I thought to myself. What now?

I was ten feet away from the veranda. My fingers buried deep into the dirt, I tried to pull myself closer. The weight of dry, dusty, blood-soaked clothes made the task even harder. I lifted my body one step at a time until I ended up at the deck of the veranda. Exhausted, that is where I stayed.

Morning broke, my lips dry and my eyes sore from the dust and grime. Feeling weak, I found it hard to raise my head from the boards. I rolled onto my back and wet my mouth with water from the dog bowl.

"You right there, mate?" I hear.

It was Merv, the mail contractor. He was a solid bloke we nicknamed 'Bull'. It wasn't just his stature but the yarns he told would get you in. Once he started he would talk for hours.

"Bull!" I yelled. "I need help." I spoke with a coarse almost whisper of a voice.

"Shit mate, what happened? I will be back," Bull replied.

Around the front he ran and drove his old dodge van back to the veranda. Shooting out of the vehicle, with his feet hardly touching the ground, the big bastard lifted me over his shoulder and carried me to the van. He opened the door and threw me on the mail bags in one heavy, but gentle, sweep closing the doors. He said, "Hang on mate, I will get you to the doc!"

The ride in the van was harsh but I was glad to finally be on the way to medical treatment. I don't know what I was worried about more: my injuries or surviving the drive.

Unable to speak, I was passing out for a while. I didn't even know where Merv was taking me. I must have been asleep for ages. It was the only way I found to block the pain. Looking out the window, I saw street power poles.

I knew we were heading for Longreach as the poles out our way were only a four by four post with a single wire.

Going in and out of consciousness, I felt every beat of my heart thumping through my veins. We came to a screaming halt. I folded in half as the mail bags compacted me against the mesh barrier inside the van. I could hear Bull yelling, "Get out here, you mongrels! I need help!" He was a man of few words and the ones he used were not very cultured but straight to the point.

Two doctors and a nurse came rushing out. I could just make out there shapes as I was lifted onto a trolley bed and that is about all I remember.

My heavy eyelids open to bright lights in what appeared to be a motel room. Confused for a moment, Merv hit my arm with his hand in a 'come on shithead, wake up' kind of way. Puzzled, my now wide eyes viewed my surroundings. Nope, defiantly not a motel room. Bloody noise everywhere, as the medical staff ran to my bed pushing buttons and poking and prodding my chest and arms. I tried to talk but couldn't the tube down my throat felt like I had tried to swallow a tree. Looking at the faces they eventually got clearer not much expression on any of them. A stuffed shirt bunch, I thought.

It seemed like half a day they buggerised around and fussed over me. Finally, Bull came back in sight.

"Well you getting a bit spoilt there, ain't ya Jo?"

Nodding my head to reply, I just listened as the big man told me how he never left my side for the past three days since he brought me here.

"Shit!" I thought to myself. I hardly know this bloke.

How does a stranger stop his world to keep an eye on another stranger? I guess the country life brings that out in you when things happen.

Later that day, the doctor removed the tube down my throat. Feeling sore, I was taking in some air and the numb feeling was fading away. I thanked Merv and we talked for a while until eventually the big fellow took off.

"I had better get Monday's mail out of the van," he laughed for today was Thursday. He walked away shaking his head with a grin on his face.

Strangely, it all went quiet. I was alone. Using my arms to lift my head above the pillow, I seen a frame across the bed restricting me from moving higher up the bed.

The nurse came in to do my meds. I asked if I could sit up and I heard the doctor's voice.

"Definitely not!"

Short and sweet but firm. Moving my head side to side, I was abusing the nurse to vent my anger. A couple of other staff members came into the room and I felt a jab from a needle then the next thing, I was falling asleep!

The next day seem to take forever. I called for a container as I needed a piss real bad, I got no reply.

"Shit!" I said. "Useless pricks, where are you?"

Lifting myself up, I noticed the frame across my legs had been removed. Good, I thought, dragging my ass up the bed.

Moving my body closer to the edge of the bed, I was going to the toilet whether they like it or not. Feeling a bit unsteady, I turned my pelvis to let my legs hang over the edge, lowering myself to the floor. Trying to stand, I lost my grip and fell head first to the floor. Laying there, I watched feet rushing in to get me back on the bed. Feeling bloody stupid, I pissed my pants in the process. The nurse and the doctor came in telling me off.

The nurse said, "We will get you out of those wet clothes," and with that my clothing came off.

"What the fuck!" I screamed. "What have you done with my leg?"

Frantically, I threw my hands on my head, feeling another needle jab. This time I felt powerless but still aware of my surroundings.

"Didn't anyone tell him?" I heard whispers.

As I lay in the bed I knew my life as a ringer had ended. No more mustering, working the property or any of the things that makes a country boy's life exciting. I heard the rain start and rattle the old corrugated roof. It started off slowly, then it pounded like a stampede of cattle. It gave me time to think. I removed the sheet that covered my legs and started to look at the mess I had acquired from the tremendous ordeal. My left leg had a bandage just above the knee, but my right leg was missing from the knee down. It was a shock and I felt ill. I laid back down on the pillow, feeling cheated of the life I had. A hell of a racket come from down the hall. It was Terry the Romanian, firing on all four cylinders. I heard feet running towards my door. The first one in was Dave.

"Fucking hell!" He yelled.

Then Terry and Noat followed in.

"What happened?" Noat said, looking at my missing lower limb. Terry, who never said much, was pale and turned away. Dave just stood there with his mouth open.

"There goes the peace and quiet," I said to the bloke in the bed beside me, still feeling weary. Time stood still as the trio came to terms with my damaged condition.

We talked for a while. It was good to have familiar faces around. I asked about Jack, but apparently the day I was injured Dave received a call from a hostel in Blackall where Jack had been. This lead Dave on a wild goose chase around Jericho and Alpha, but still no sign of Jack.

Dave had only become aware of me being in hospital when Merv the postal contractor turned up at the house.

They gathered themselves and came directly here to the hospital. Merv had only told them I was a bit crook, not mentioning I had almost died and lost half my bloody leg, the big lug.

Dave and Noat came to visit me a few more times over the past month. It was always good to talk about how the property was going and to rub it in that me missing made no difference at all. Yeah, sure! It was about time those lazy buggers earned their keep, I thought.

I had been getting around on crutches for a week now, not doing too badly. So I lost a leg, I thought to myself. Being an optimist, I had spent a lot of time pondering how to survive when I go back to the homestead. The doc came in and told me I could go home as long as someone was there to care for me.

So I replied, "Yep, me mates are coming to get me this arvo!"

It was about two o'clock when I got to get out of that place. Crutches under my arms and my swag over my left shoulder, I took off out of the hospital. I said goodbye to the staff briefly as they were working flat out. Once on the street, the light in my eyes was blinding me until I adjusted. Slowly but surely, I moved down the sidewalk.

It was a strange feeling and I felt everyone's eyes watching my every step. People I had known all my life were looking at me weirdly, knowing my life was up the shit. I walked into the old Dalgety store where Allan, the manager, had an old Holden Ute he used to let us use sometimes. Allan was up in the loft getting some equipment.

I yelled out, "Hey Al, is it alright if I borrow the Ute?"

His voice from above called back to me, "Yeah sure, Jo!"

The keys were always in the car so I staggered my way through the shop to where the Ute was parked.

"How the bloody hell do I drive? Ah, bugger it!" I thought. "Can't be too hard!"

As I opened the door to the cab of the Ute, I threw the crutches into the tray and hopped to the side of the opening. Leaning on the roof, I swung my ass towards the seat. Fuck! Missed. I reached up and got back on my feet. Oh, should I say my foot now? All set to try again, I finally land on the seat. I move across and swing my leg in. Being a manual gearbox in the old HR Holden, it was a challenge knowing I couldn't use the clutch. It felt strange as I pumped the accelerator and started the car. I warmed it up then turned it off. Placing the car into first gear, I released the handbrake and started the car with no clutch. It shuddered and jolted me as it moved forward a few revs and I was on the way down the driveway.

I idled down the road until I was able to change the car into second by using the revs. Unable to use the clutch, I thought I'd stay in second for a while until I got out of the Main Street of Longreach and I turned past the old fuel storage depot.

"I can do it," I thought to myself, as I attempted to get into third. It was not so easy, but a few harsh grinds and it was in, bouncing about like a jack rabbit. The Ute sped up and I was making progress. About a half hour into the drive I saw the local copper had gone into the soft edge of the road and was stuck. He was trying to flag me down as I went flying past. It took me ages to get going, I was not going to stop for anyone. I could see an old dodge truck coming towards me, he was bound to stop and help so I kept my foot on the throttle.

I was feeling tired as I came across the homestead track. Still in top gear I swung in at about thirty miles an hour. The ass of the Ute tracking out into the gravel. I was home. Arriving at the homestead, I went to slow down, but confusing the peddles. It was an awkward mix up. I didn't know how to stop. Dave and Terry were at the stable when I crashed into the shed, hitting the tractor so hard it fell off the stand where it was being repaired. Steam pouring out of the radiator, I opened the door. "I'm home!" I yelled, trying to stand using my hands to move out of the shed. I was laughing with pain and was delighted to be back.

CHAPTER FOUR

It has been a few weeks since my surprise arrival back home. Sitting here, just drinking rum and strumming the old guitar. Noat was watching me all the time, smothering me like I was a wounded puppy. It was getting unbearable, having to ask if I could go to the bathroom or even just to go outside. I needed to get out in the yard and look, even if I cannot do anything else. I reached for my crutches, but Noat grasped them tight.

"Where do you think you're going?"

He pushed me back down in the chair.

"Piss off, you mongrel! I'm going outside," I said, raising myself onto the floor. I began hopping to the front door.

Once outside, I looked back and Noat had thrown my crutches in disgust over the other side of the room.

"Well bugger it," I said, as I made my way down the stairs.

Wow! It was good to feel the dirt beneath my feet. Argh! Foot! An expression that I now needed to change.

I guess you could say I mastered the art of standing on one leg very easily after the thirtieth time I fell on my ass, but eventually hugging the post of the stable to support myself. Slamming the back door, Noat went out of the house in a rage.

"Stupid prick!" He was muttering as he shot me a disgusting look followed by raising his middle finger.

Once at the stable, I moved around steadily from post to post. Old Benny, the thoroughbred, was in the stable saddled up. Terry must have been working him earlier and put him in the stable for a spell. Benny looked at me through the puzzled eyes that indicated my appearance had changed from last he seen me. I looked at the saddle knowing I was not able to ride anymore due to missing my leg. My mind was ticking over with ideas. I was determined to ride again. I looked at buckets, tins, rope and even a bird cage. How I could use a bird cage, buggered me.

I saw a bit of old down pipe that had been cut down. It was round with a ninety degree bend at the top of it. I turned it upside down. Nearby was a pair of metal shears. I began to trim the down pipe to a usable size. I had been left with a short bit of my limb just below the knee. After cutting the metals to size, I wrapped a towel around the stump and proceeded to force it into the pipe, creating a makeshift leg. Almost a perfect fit, I thought. Good enough for now.

I stood up and got my balance. Hey, I can walk again! Well, momentarily. I fell forward hitting my head on the railing. Still determined, I was once again upright moving about. It felt strange, but a feeling of achievement washed over me and it was amazing.

I headed towards Benny. He was very calm, considering the noise I made. I untied the steed and at this point I don't know if was crazy or not, but I placed my left leg into the stirrup, hoisting myself aboard. Using my hand to lift the pipe base of my leg across the saddle.

Exhausted, I surprised myself. Feeling bloody proud, I am! I moved the pipe into the right stirrup, just easing it in. I put weight upon the saddle mounts to lift my butt off the seat. Even though it was cutting in to my stump, I was going for a ride no matter what. I reached over and unhitched the gate and out I walked the horse. Slow and steady, I got my bearings and moved out of the yard.

Freedom, at last. I did it! I had finally brought my sense of wellbeing to a new level.

Wandering out to the edge of the homestead and my leg was hurting, so I headed back. Moving the wrong way, suddenly my downpipe replacement fell off onto the ground.

Shit! I thought to myself. This will make getting down fun. But at least it wasn't cutting in any more.

Once I was back at the stables, I felt well balanced and confident. Lifting my bum off the seat, I was feeling pretty damn cocky, I tell you! Nothing could spoil my day. I moved steadily towards the fence with the idea of using the rails to hold me solid whilst I got down. A car was making its way down the drive so I stayed on the saddle rather than have the horse move as I climbed off.

I went on to greet the vehicle. Wow! It was Julie it had been ages since I saw her last. My heart was pounding like a jack hammer.

"Hello Jo!" She yelled out of the window.

I smiled and remained cool so I didn't lose my balance. I pulled alongside of the driver's side window with my good leg out so I didn't frighten her away. We spoke for a while then decided to go back to the house.

Once back at the house, I lifted my body off the saddle doing the typical cowboy descend. Although once in the air, it dawned on me. You only got one leg, you bloody fool! No time to think, I landed on my foot, twisting it as I tumbled to the ground like a falling limb of a tree. Swearing my head off with the pain, sending sharp jolts through my legs.

"Fuck!" I screamed and called out.

At least I only twisted one ankle. I grinned, biting my teeth hard. Julie came to help me but I shoved her away.

"Don't be stupid," she said. "You're only lame. If you were a horse, I would shoot you!"

Well, what could I say? Of all the romantic things I have ever heard in my life, that touched my heart the deepest. I think I will have to marry this girl.

"Come on then. Help me up, you sarcastic bitch!"

Shaking my head. For a little bugger, she was strong. Lifting me to my feet and helping me into the homestead.

"Noat told me you lost your leg in an accident but he didn't tell me you also lost your mind. What were you doing on that bloody horse?" She cursed me all the way to the lounge room where I sat down. I didn't hesitate, I kissed her on the lips.

"I love you," I said. Julie stood up. She looked really disappointed in me. Tears were rolling down her face.

"Oh, shit! What have I done!"

Julie stood there quietly, looking at me. I couldn't get out of the chair. I was worried. I called out to Terry, who was in the kitchen.

He walked into the room and with a deep voice he replied, "What's up?"

"I don't know. Julie won't move or talk to me. Give her a shake or something mate. I think she is in shock or something like that."

"Hey! Snap out of it." he yelled. "Hey, woman!" He touched her on the shoulder and Julie fell into his arms, crumbling like a train wreck.

"Jo asked me to marry him!" She screamed, alerting everyone in a hundred mile radius.

Hang on, I thought back.

Nope. I don't remember that. Going back over what I said, there was definitely no mention of marriage in my mind. Within the next few minutes more people than I had seen in the past three months were coming in the door, congratulating Julie and

I. This time I was holding Julie in my arms with a stunned expression on my face.

I don't know what to do. If I say I didn't ask her, then I might lose her for good. And I guess I did have a thought in my head about the fact I should marry this girl, who knows maybe I did ask her.

Me, of all people, cannot ever think of a time where marriage was something I had even contemplated in my life time. I reckon Julie is a greater influence on my life than I had ever considered her to be.

The event settled down and Terry cooked a special meal in our honour. Noat and Dave had sat down.

I didn't even see Merv in the house until we sat down to eat. I was unaware he was here. But it's typical though, if there is a free feed, he would find it.

It felt good after all that has happened that my injuries were second on my mind. I just wanted to hold Julie tight as the sun went down over the dusty plains.

Three months had past eventually I was able to buy Julie an engagement ring. Bloody hell! I could have bought a Ute for that amount of cash, but to see the smile on my girl's face it was worth every cent.

The coming months brought a new start in my life. I was fitted with a prosthesis and I easily managed the art of walking. I felt human and useful around the property again. The wet season had just begun so working on the land had its disadvantages but it gave us time to repair the yards. The ground was softer and a fence post went in easier.

Early one evening, we were settling down for a late supper and lights appeared outside the stables, down towards the front gates. We watched the vehicle as it made its way to the homestead. A flash looking car appeared.

"It's one of those stretchy thinga-me-bobs!" Merv let go in his usual loud mouth way.

"Strewth!" He said as the car came into light. It pulled up near the stairs. Looking like a mob of galahs, we watched as the door opened.

"Knock me down with a feather!" Noat exclaimed, as Jack poked his head out.

"What's up? Haven't you ever seen a superstar before?" He laughed.

Merv in his unwitty ways went and held the door and curtsied as Jack stepped from the limo.

"Crikey!" Called Dave. "Did ya rob a bank, Jack?"

"No," he replied. "Just finally used my head, not my brawn. When I left town, I shot off to Brissie, only to find myself without a place to live. Then I met Tony Deighton. He is the local man that knows everything about everything, if you know what I mean!"

"So come on, you little rat bag! Tell us what you been doing," said Big Merv, all excited as he passed Jack a beer.

When the morning broke, the homestead looked like a disaster zone. Somehow we had more empty beer bottles than cattle. Julie lifted her head first, taking a good look around and decided to put her head back down and pretend she was out of it but the sound of five large men snoring was like a freight train holding yard.

"Bugger it!" she said, as she got up and placed the kettle on the wood stove. Whilst outside cutting kindling to start the fire, Julie saw a truck at the loading ramp. There were three men shuffling the herd into trailers. Thinking the boys had organised a big shift from one yard to another, she went inside and lit the fire. Noat raised his ugly head and staggered around the house, awkwardly stumbling into the kitchen. The stove heated up the cold, country air. Julie addressed Noat by saying good morning and stated the men have kicked off early this morning.

"What do ya mean?" Replied Noat.

"Just when I was chopping wood, the truck was being loaded with the cattle!" She exclaimed.

"What!" Noat yelled at the top of his voice waking up everyone from their sleep. He ran outside to see the truck disappear out the roadway. It was like a stampede as everyone stormed off the veranda into the vehicles by the shed. Jack went out back to get the trail bike and sped on after the others. Julie puzzled by all the excitement had no idea of cattle rustlers and there dawn raids which have been occurring in the area. Terry had his faithful Winchester, 'Betty', beside him as the sleep dissolved form his eyes. Dave and Merv were in the four wheel drive. The Ute lifted high off the ground as it made flight across the rugged landscape. Julie and myself left the property and took chase along the roadway closing in on the truck eventually tailgating the trailer trying to work out how we get past the dust on the road blinding our sight.

A gunshot rang out. Merv had a shot at the truck, the bullet collecting the cabin mirror as it went through making the driver swerve from one side of the road to the other. I stepped on the brakes hard as we hit the back of the trailer almost sending us flying into the gully.

Taking a moment to compose, we took off catching up to the truck again. This time keeping enough distance.

Meanwhile, Julie was looking very pale and holding onto the door handle ready to bolt if she got a chance, I think.

Merv and Dave, who were full of fury, went crashing through the boundary fence and in the path of the cattle rustlers. Somehow, I think, the look on Merv's face had convinced them that he was serious about shooting them again so the truck came to a halt. By the time the dust had cleared, Terry was standing with the tip of his rifle on the bridge of the driver's nose.

Meanwhile, the passenger had jumped out and starting running across the field, and you guessed it, Jack was in pursuit in his own crazy way. Standing on the seat of the motorbike, Jack looked like a pro as he leaped onto the back of the unfortunate bloke he was chasing, throwing him to the ground and roping him as if it was a steer in for branding.

Jack, proud as punch, was standing on top of the offender, waving his arms and holding his hat high to show off his handy work. Dave went over and gave Jack a hand to throw the rustler in the back of the Ute and brought them back to the truck. Merv was sitting on the driver, posing with his catch, but leaving the poor bloke underneath gasping for air. He was losing consciousness with Merv's large build weighing down on top.

"Get off him, you big bugger!" I said. "Geez, we don't want to bury them yet!"

"Who the bloody hell are you and what is going on?" Terry yelled, as he cocked the rifle. Knowing that the closest police station around here was a hundred miles away, we had to take control of the situation in the country. Taking the law into your own hands does not come with a rule book, so we done the best we could.

Not a word was spoken, we all waited for the men to reply. Nothing.

"You can all take the truck back to the homestead and let the cattle back in the yard. I will take care of these blokes," Terry said in a tone that meant he was not kidding around.

Julie fainted at the thought of what Terry would do, so we lifted the bike into the Ute along with Julie. She would have freaked to know how she got home.

I started the truck up and headed on my way to turn around as Merv and Dave headed back to fix the boundary fence. Heading back to where I left Terry with the two men, I saw that a police vehicle had arrived. The young Constable was trying to convince Terry to back off and let him take them in, but as usual, the big Romanian's stubborn attitude had taken hold. I felt sorry for the copper as I drove by leaving them to sort out the standoff between the law of the land and the law of justice.

The last of the cattle were unloaded and I parked the rig. I went inside, only to be hit in the head by a coffee cup. Blood flowing down my face from the cut above my eye, I ducked as another projectile was on the way. The vision of an outraged woman stood in my path. I guess Julie was not happy about her trip back to the homestead.

After an hour and thirty plates and ten cups, Julie settled down. It was lucky we only had thirty plates and ten cups or she would still be going. I left the house and went to the yards, giving Julie time to settle.

The police paddy wagon turned into the driveway with the two criminals walking behind tethered to the tow bar.

Terry was in the passenger seat. I saw that he and the officer had come to an agreement on how to handle the situation. The men were weary from there walk, but Terry and the copper had a few beers whilst making their way back and were a bit under the weather. It was not unlikely to have a drink around these parts, even if you were wearing a uniform.

We took turns at writing statements for the Constable to take with him about the event. Locking the prisoners in the paddy wagon for him and placing him in the front seat. We were unable to offer him a coffee to sober him up due to the fact we don't have any cups now, thanks to Julie.

I asked Terry if he got them to talk but they never said a word, so we were still in the dark. Hopefully the police will have better luck.

It was getting late and the whole day was taken up by what had happened. Merv was on the couch on the front veranda snoring his head off. I am under the impression he forgot he doesn't live here. It is costing a fortune to feed the big fella. Dave and Jack were running the cattle out of the yards and into the pasture. Terry was muttering about the copper spoiling his fun, whilst Noat was trying to get on the party line to contact Dalgety about the upcoming sale in Longreach next week, but old Maureen had the line congested.

We were hoping to cash in some of the cattle to keep the property afloat, and although things were going well, you cannot take it for granted. The country side is dry, the water holes are merely a crater in the dust, whilst the cattle are struggling to survive. The cattle sales would be a big relief as the pregnant heifers were due to calf over the coming months.

CHAPTER FIVE

The week had gone fast and Noat had decided which cattle were going to the sales next week.

"Should get good money for these old grass recyclers," he said. We were lucky to have them after the drama last week.

Merv arrived back from his mail run. His old van was running a bit rough, so he headed straight out to the tractor shed to work on it.

Tagging the cattle for sale was always Noat's responsibility. He picked which ones would go. Set with his hand bag, as we called it, just to hear him bite. We won't see him for the rest of the day. Jack's voice came from the stables, followed by a little chuckle from Dave.

Julie and I were finally on speaking terms again after I threw her in the back of the Ute, unconscious, last week. Something that I won't be forgiven for, for a while. Talking to Julie on the front veranda, the sound of a car coming down the driveway was heard. As I turned around, a police car, followed by two other cars, pulled up near the stables. We were not expecting any visitors today, so this was out of the ordinary. The young Constable was the first to step out of the police car, followed by the Longreach Senior Sergeant Peter Ingles. I could see Jack and Dave sticking their heads out of the rails, but lost sight of Jack when the police lifted the hats to their heads. This is never a good sign.

The other cars were sitting back a little way, as if to assess the situation before leaving the vehicles. Constable Taylor walked closer and requested they spoke to Jack.

"It has something to do with the cattle incident last week," he exclaimed.

It was then that four men out of each of the other cars stepped out and into view. Two of them were the cattle rustlers we caught last week. I could feel the tension grow as Terry came from out the back shed where he and Merv were fixing the mail truck. He stormed forward like a Mallee bull. Terry was furious.

"Hold up there, you stupid pig-headed clown! Let me sort it out before you get us all locked up."

"Come on in," I said to the coppers. "And we can talk."

But they both stood firm and told me to get Jack, who was nowhere to be found.

Dave said, "What has my brother done now?!" Shaking his head.

"Well it seems like these blokes own the cattle they were loading into the truck last week!" The Senior Sergeant said in a powerful and arrogant tone that made us take note and listen.

"I will go and get Noat before we go any further. It's his property and his cattle," Julie said nervously.

A short time later, Noat and Julie appeared. Noat was briefed on what the coppers said. He was not happy at all and wanted to get to the bottom of the problem.

"When Jack left and went to Brisbane eight months ago, he had accumulated a lot of bad debts to some high profile businessmen. He used the cattle on the station as collateral and these men are debt collectors. They have papers to take 100 head of cattle, according to these documents."

"Bullshit!" Noat blurted out. "You're not touching my herds! Jack has no rights to them, and neither do you."

Taking the paperwork from the police, I began to read them

silently. Everyone waited until I had gone through them.

"Maybe you should read this," I said as I passed Noat the bad news.

Jack somehow was the owner of the Caplin Station brand. Taking the papers from my hand, Noat, in a rage, screamed his head off, "That bastard!"

About ten years ago when Noat cut off his toes, he was in hospital. So Jack was sent to register the brand. Along the way, Jack had a few too many drinks and lost the original authorisation form. So when he eventually made it into town, he had to fill out new ones with his own name so the brand could be registered by that afternoon. Noat had known about this, but never thought anything of it. But now it has come back to bite him on the ass.

"No! This is not right!" Noat yelled.

"JACK!"

"JACK!"

"Get here now!"

Noat's voice echoed across the yards, stirring the cattle and causing them to break free towards the police and the other men. The noise made them all jump back into the cars, as the herd went stampeding past. Noat could do nothing to stop them, so he ran up onto the veranda.

There were at least sixty head that he had cut from the others whilst sorting them for the sale. These were the bad conditioned beasts that he set to go to the doggers. Unable to get the gate closed, Dave stood in the empty yard as the dust settled. The cows headed up the driveway onto to the road, slowly the windows went down in the cars.

"THERE YOU GO!" Noat yelled out. "There's your hundred head. Go and catch the mongrels yourself, and get off my land!"

Eager to get their pound of flesh, the men took off after them disappearing out of sight. Noat handed the officers the paperwork and asked them to countersign his signature.

Looking at each other, the Sergeant said, "Sounds good to me."

The deal was made.

"I didn't care much for those blokes anyway," he said.

"But keep that bloody Jack under control. I thought we had seen the last of him. I am not happy he is back."

The coppers scrambled back to the car and took off. We looked high and low for Jack, but could not find him anywhere.

Skinny little bugger hides better than a bloody bilby. Terry and Merv had finished repairs on the van. It was running sweet as a nut and finished it just in time for dinner. Everybody went to the old tank behind the house to wash their hands before going inside. It was common to strip off naked and washing all over at the end of the day, but just a quick hand wash would suffice as the feed was ready.

Inside, Julie and Terry were serving the tucker on a few old plates taken from the cottages on the ridge. There were also coffee cups on the tables and that was strange seeing as we had none left since Julie lost the plot a week ago. Heading up the back stairs, we could see Jack sitting high in the seat. Somehow he had slipped under the radar when we searched for him.

"Just been to Maddison Cottage and got some dishes," he said.

"How was your day?" Jack continued with a smirk on his face as if he didn't know what had happened.

Noat took off his boot and like a flash of lightning and threw it, clobbering Jack right between the eyes and knocking him off the chair. If looks could kill there would be one less place setting at the table, but a good steak was waiting, and we learnt to never hold off eating.

First things first, Jack will get sorted out later. With everyone seated at the table, Merv asked Jack for the salt shaker. Jack then passed it to Noat, who used it and within seconds of using it, it went flying past Jack's head. It was a very tense and unstable atmosphere.

With dinner done, Merv grabbed Jack and took him out of reach of Noat, who was making a bee line at the skinny runt. This was a good move on Merv's behalf, because Noat was wild and spent the entire night glaring out the window to the veranda where Jack was sitting.

The country living relies on a trust and bond unlike any other, although we had lost approximately sixty head of cattle due to Jack's shonky dealings. At the end of the day, Noat didn't have to cart the animals he had no use for off to the doggers. The fuel for the truck normally cost more than he got for them.

On the morning mail run, Merv had come across a couple of old wheels which he placed in his van. The tyres were good, so out to the shed he went, asking Jack to give him a hand. Standing up, Merv lifted his big carcass too fast and Jack tumbled ass up on the floor just as Noat walked in the door.

"Don't care how much you kiss my feet Jack, I am still pissed off with you!"

Noat chuckled once again. Jack was quick enough to avoid a good swift kick to the head as Noat swung his foot forward.

"Bugger!" Noat complained.

The wheels in the van had brand new tread.

"What are they off?" Terry asked, looking over the gate into the shed.

"I don't know," said Merv. "Could be off a trailer or something like that. I found them near Rodents Creek Bridge. Thought we might be able to use them. I will put them in the loft."

The next morning was cold and wet. The rain had made its way from up north. This was a welcoming sight. Dave and Jack were out checking the yards, whilst Terry and Noat fixed the broken gate to the yard. I waited for Julie to get ready, as we were heading into town for supplies. I woke Merv up, who was asleep on the veranda and then headed down to start the car.

Our fuel was stored in a tank high on the stand. Not power operated, just gravity fed. I drove over and topped the Ute up for the journey into town. About ten gallons should be enough to do the trip. Julie finally came out to the car and got in, looking at me as if to say, 'Hurry up. What are you waiting for?' Go figure!

The road was slippery and the dust had turned to mud. Traction was very poor but steadily we went. Julie kept an eye out as well, and between the both of us our one hour trip took two hours.

Jundah was only a small town, so not a lot of choices for shopping. But this month the supplies would be slim.

"Just the basics," I said to Julie as she headed in the store. I waited outside. Allan, our mate from Longreach who owns the Dalgety store, was talking to the local mayor. I overheard them saying a family was missing, a man and woman with three children. The police have no leads to their whereabouts.

I entered their conversation with, "Hello fellas, what's this I hear about someone missing?"

"Yeah. A family, Jo," Allan replied. "Mick was just filling me in with the latest on them. Still no word though. They were last seen travelling from Longreach to Jundah, but never made it. Do you know anything about it?"

"No," I replied. "This is the first I had heard."

I made my way into the pub to wait for Julie. I ordered myself a longneck bottle. I liked to save on glasses around here. Soon after I downed the last bottle, Julie arrived. Oops! I have seen that look before. Julie stamped her feet and told me to put the groceries in the car.

"Bloody women! Can't a bloke have a drink anymore?" I replied.

We left Jundah and were on the way back to Caplin Station. Travelling along the road, we approached Rodent Creek, the bridge where Merv found the wheels. For some reason I felt obliged to stop. I don't know what it was, some sort of strange feeling. Out of the car, I walked towards the edge of the creek. There was nothing there. I didn't have a clue what I was looking for but my hairs were standing on end and my legs trembled as I went to the other side to look.

Nothing there either. I relaxed and shrugged my shoulders to let Julie know I had found nothing. Walking back to the car, I decided to look under the bridge just to fill my curiosity.

"What the!" I yelled as I caught a glimpse of a car and caravan upside down directly below the bridge. I told Julie to drive back to Jundah to get help. I started making my way down the slippery embankment. I took one step then fell on my ass and landed in the creek beside the overturned wreck, losing my prosthesis in the water.

Finding a branch to get myself to a firm foot hold, I moved towards the car. The front windscreen was in the water but I could see the passenger's shoulders poking out, but the head was beneath the surface. I did not hold much hope for the driver so I went to the back door. Looking inside, I saw no one else but the driver and passenger.

I could do nothing to help, it was too late for these two. The caravan was torn apart from the impact and resembled a shoe box being crushed for the bin. My lips were dry and I headed back to the road as I waited for Julie to return with help. About half an hour had passed before the ambulance and police arrived, closely followed by Julie.

"No good," I said. "No survivors."

We helped as much as we could but left the authorities to deal with it. Exhausted, I let Julie drive. I felt weary and a bit drained. It is never good to find deceased accident victims.

After we arrived back at home, the police turned up. And once again, Jack went missing. They came to tell us that the car belonged to the family that was missing but the children have disappeared and they wanted us to help in the search. Jack peered around the corner with a guilty look.

"Relax, Jack. They are here looking for volunteers to look for some missing kids."

Jack, Noat and Terry decided to go and search, leaving Julie and myself to clean up and finish putting the supplies away.

I attempted to phone Longreach so Merv can keep a look out on his way back to the property. But as usual, Maureen would not pick up in the telephone exchange.

Grabbing my crutches and unable to find my false leg, I headed to the old shed. There was a long range radio which had not been used for years. I hoped I might get it going to talk to someone in town to pass on a message on to Merv.

Taking the battery out of the Ute, I found some wire to get the radio working.

"Caplin Station to anybody in Longreach," I repeated my request a number of times with no luck, until I got a reply from Constable Taylor at the Longreach Police Station.

"Hello," I said. "I want to leave a message for Merv, the mail contractor. He should be at the post office."

"Okay," the Constable said. "Merv was just here. I will just grab him, he can't be too far."

About ten minutes went by, then the sound of big Merv's voice shook the speakers. I told Merv that the police were looking for three young children and the car they were in had ran off the Rodent Creek Bridge.

"What do these kids look like?" He replied. "Over."

"I am not sure. The police were not clear. Why?"

"Well, Maureen has her grandchildren at the moment. Their parents have gone travelling for a few days. The officer is right beside me. He is on the phone to Maureen, as we speak. Over."

I stood quietly, lost for words. I left the shed and returned back inside. I wanted to tell Julie what Merv had said but I didn't. I just hoped that the children were safe.

A few hours had passed since I spoke with Merv. I tried the telephone again, but nothing. It was unsettling, not knowing about the situation with the missing children.

I began to daze out the window when a car approaching the house came into my view. It was the young Constable in his private car.

"G'day!" He said, as he stepped out of the car. "Just stopped in to let you know that the people under the bridge were Maureen's son and daughter in law. She has the children and they are okay. The search was ended about an hour ago. Thanks for your help. The boys are at Jundah pub, sinking a few cold ones."

"That's great. Thank you." I called out, feeling a bit better but also sad for the kids.

The copper got back in his car and headed off. I turned to Julie and hugged her tight.

"Fair go!" She stepped back and hit me across the face. Feeling a bit stunned, I couldn't work out what I had done.

"What did I do to deserve that?"

"Because I am still angry with you, shithead! Besides, don't go getting soft on me now, you whimp! Now, get off your ass and chop some wood for the fire place. I am making a roast for dinner."

Boy, talk about hardening up. I think I created a monster. It's true though, the only way to get back on track is to face reality. No time to be weak.

I took off out the back door, hopping on one leg down to the timber box. I tell you what, it took the stuffing out of me. I had gotten used to having my prosthesis and with it gone, it has taken my co-ordination and most of my strength to get around. I started chopping the kindling for the fire, balancing to the best of my ability. I filled up the wood cart and wheeled it inside.

As I reached the top of the stairs, Julie came running out, hugging and kissing me. Startled, I couldn't move.

"What's going on with you? You silly woman!" I said.

"Nothing. I want you. I want you bad," she giggled.

I don't know what got into her but I wasn't going to knock it back. I raced off to the room.

A great afternoon with Julie was exactly what I needed.

Later on that evening, we were sitting on the couch listening to a bit of Elvis when Noat and the others turned up drunk as skunks.

"Go and wash up," I told them. "Julie's cooked a roast, so you better eat it!"

The meal went down well. It takes more than a gut full of grog to stop these blokes from pigging out. I went to move away from the table lifting myself up so I could hop into the kitchen.

I heard Jack talking to Dave saying, "Are you going to give it to him?"

"What are you talking about?" I replied. Dave shook his head and said "Nuffin'."

Washing the dishes is always a good way to take away the stress of the day, but my afternoon was stress-free. I smiled at Julie.

The rain had disappeared. The night sky looked like it had been washed, the moon was big and clouds were scarce. The faint sunset on the horizon had a red glow, and it enlightened the twilight essence. It felt romantic. Julie and I discussed a time and place for our wedding. We didn't want to rush into it, but the date was set for March 24, approximately 10 months away. The location would be at her family property, a place she had not revisited since Casper Norton killed her parents and brothers. I did not know if this was a good idea, but Julie felt it would be the best place and the only way she could move on to the future.

Early the next morning, I took Julie's BMW for a drive to Blackall. I left before anyone else stirred. The thought of the wedding bugged me all night, so I went to check the house out. A gut feeling brewed my senses to a degree that my stomach would not settle.

Blackall is a rather big town and the people were down to earth and always friendly. I had never been to Julie's home before, as it was never on my list of places to visit.

I stopped at the local library and asked if anyone knew where the old Archer property was located. A deadly silence swept across the room. I could feel eyes burning the back of my neck.

"The Archer place. Does anyone know where it is?" I asked.

"Who wants to know?" Bellowed a voice from down an aisle in the fiction section.

"My name is Jo, and I am engaged to Julie Archer. I just want to see the house as Julie would like to come back here for our exchanging of vows, and if the place is up to it, possibly have the wedding there."

"Why didn't you say?! Come here. And where is Julie?"

I was almost crushed as well wishes embraced me. No sooner had one person let go, another had hold of my hand, shaking it. My fingers started losing sensations. Somehow I ended up on the steps to the library.

"Julie doesn't know I was on my way here, so she is still at Caplin Station, where we are staying." I said, concerned that someone would spill the beans.

"I know that place!" One of the older fellows replied. "You boys are looking after it whilst the old man is in jail, aren't you?"

"Well, umm… Noat actually owns the property now. It was given to him by his father a while back."

"Jump in your car Jo, and follow us."

Once in the car, my nerves caused me to shake. I am actually feeling nervous now and afraid the house's condition would be too bad now I have gotten the local folks all excited. About two miles out we turned left along a freshly painted timber fence. All you could see was white fence for miles, but it seemed to disappear over the rise. The fence was massive and once I looked over it, I could see a big motel or something similar.

Cool, I thought to myself. That would make a good landmark for when guests come to Julie's house further on or where ever it is.

By now there were close to twelve cars following us. Most of the library had taken off to follow us out.

The lead car stopped at a gate with a cobblestone driveway which made its way up to the motel. The gate was locked so the big bloke who first spoke to me unlocked it and waved me through. I went around the car in front and pulled up beside him.

"What are we doing here?" I asked. Then I saw a sign behind

him that read 'Archer Station'.

"The biggest station in Blackall. My name is Gavin. The town has kept the property going since the loss of the Archer family. They were pioneers of this area and we have rebuilt the station for Julie hoping she would return one day."

I went ahead, driving slow as if I was trespassing. The closer I got, the bigger the house grew. Three stories high, I had never been to a place this enormous. It was eerie knowing that the family had been slaughtered here, but it also looked brand new. The smell of fresh paint filled the air as I got out and grabbed my crutches.

There were marble steps leading up to the entrance. I could not look up as the building was so high. The movie 'Giant' with Rock Hudson and James Dean came into my head. That is the only recollection I have of seeing a house of this stature, but this bugger is huge.

I gulped before taking the first step onto the huge landing. Then other cars had started to make their way to where I had parked. The locals were standing by them applauding as I made my way up the steps.

I stopped and turned back, heading down the stairs to the car.

"What's up mate? Where are you going?" Gavin asked, worried.

"Sorry, but it's not my place. I cannot go inside. It does not feel right. Julie needs to be the one to return here when she feels like it."

I got back in the car and drove away from these strangers.

"When are you coming back?" They yelled as I put my foot down on the accelerator.

It was late afternoon when I reached Caplin Station and Julie came out to greet me.

"Where did you go today, Jo?"

"I had to see the blokes at Dalgety in Longreach about the cattle sale tomorrow."

Noat being very quick witted said, "Oh, yeah. That's right, Jo. How is it all going? I just sent the trucks in there about an hour ago. Thanks for doing the running around for me."

"How come I didn't know about this?" Julie asked.

"I told you the other day, remember?" Hoping Julie didn't catch onto my lies.

Not wanting to feel out of place, Julie replied, "Oh, now I remember!"

Then a, "Sure!" was heard as she whispered under her breath.

The next day was taken up by the sales in Longreach. We headed out early and blended in with the crowd. It was common to have some bogus bidders. It was a day full of adrenalin, every time a bid would hit the reserve, we raised it just enough for the price to go over. The more we did this, the better the profits would be.

I never mentioned to Julie about going to Blackall, but it was still in the back of my mind.

"Thirsty work calls for a drink!" I said. So Julie and I headed to the bar for a break. Sitting down to a cold beer, the woman behind the counter said, "You're Julie Archer, aren't ya?"

"Yes," Julie replied.

"I met Jo yesterday in Blackall. Congratulations on the engagement!"

"Bazza! I yelled, then I grabbed Julie by the hand and cut the conversation short.

"What was that all about, Jo?" Julie yelled at the top of her voice.

Wow! Talk about stopping time. There was a deadly silence.

Her fierce and forceful attitude sent most men to water.

"How you going, Barry? I don't know if you met Julie yet."

Trying to ignore her whilst everyone else went back to the business at hand, drinking and yearning about the good old days. I had not seen Bazza for eight years. Last time we set eyes on each other I gave him black ones, but this was the only decoy I could find.

Bazza was a smooth character and he knew how to swoon the women. Soon he had Julie mesmerised with his charm. We talked for a while then made our way back to the auction ring. Most of Noat's cattle were sold. This was good, he was over the moon and letting everyone know it.

Jack and Dave turned up with Terry. They had been casting an eye on the steers in the other yards. The call for the auction to start in a private yard came over the loud speaker. This was only top quality cattle, so if you weren't invited to bid, then you were not allowed. The best cattle were sourced for the most exclusive clientele.

"Last call for Archer Station Bidders!" The voice beamed through the loudspeakers. I looked at Julie, as tears ran down her face. The sound of the family station made her feel ill and down to the floor she fell.

"Make room!" I yelled, as I tried to get Julie to come to. Noat lifted her up in his arms, carrying her into the open. Jack had moved some hay bales for Noat to lay her down. Dave had some water, so I wet her lips slowly. Julie came back around, a bit groggy and pail. She sat up and apologised for her passing out.

"Can we go home?" said Julie. "I need to get away from here. That used to be my family's brand but to hear it now." She paused.

"I cannot handle someone else owning the name. I know life goes on," she said. "But it has hit me hard."

"Yes. No problem," I said.

"So who owns the property now then?" I asked.

"I wouldn't have a clue." She said. "When I left, different people were trying to claim it. I just left."

"I know," I said.

"I want to get married there, but Jo, I don't think we can. Someone else has the property now, otherwise they would not have cattle for sale."

I wanted to tell her what I had found out about the station yesterday but I was caught in this tangled web of being open or holding back.

Just as that thought passed my mind, the new Mayor of Longreach held out his hand to Julie's.

"It is good to see you here, Julie. I haven't seen you about for a while. How have you been?"

"Hello Mister Broad," Julie replied.

"Call me Alex," he said.

"Okay Alex."

"Your cattle sold well." Alex replied.

"Thanks," I said.

"No. Not you. Julie."

Julie, taken aback by what the Mayor had said, "Whatever do you mean?" She asked.

"Well you still own Archer Station. The town people of Blackall said Jo was there yesterday and seen how they have kept your property working. And I must say it is making big news around Australia and the world, congratulations!"

"Is this true? Is that what that bitch at the bar was talking about? What did you do yesterday? You lying bastard!"

Before I could say anything, I felt my eye socket sink to the back of my head as Julie's fist flattened me like a pancake.

"What right did you have to go into my family's house?"

Dave and Terry were holding Julie's arms and Jack was swinging off her legs as Julie attempted to kick me. Rolling around like a turtle on its back, I got one of my crutches and tried to get up. Just as I started to lift, bloody Julie kicked the crutch away again. It was like a standoff with a rampaging bull, it took time for Julie to settle down.

Not a word was said on the way home.

Almost an hour out of Longreach Julie said, "Turn the car around. I want you to take me back home to Blackall."

I pulled over to the edge of the road and asked her to repeat what she had said.

"You heard me. I want to see for myself what all the fuss is about," she replied.

"Okay."

So I did a u-turn and headed back the way we just came. It took about three hours to get to Blackall. I was actually feeling a bit dreary and my head was nodding off as we turned down the road to Archer Station.

"The fences! The fences!" Screamed Julie. "They have fixed the fences!"

The excitement woke me out of the semi coma I was driving in. Bouncing up and down on the seat like a playful puppy, her eyes open and almost ready to pop out. We travelled along over the rise and for the first time I saw Julie as happy as could be. She was almost delirious and told me to pull over, which I did. We stepped out of the car and Julie ran through the railings, heading towards the house. Well there was no way I could catch her with one leg and crutches so I got back in the car and made my way to the property gate. The gate was unlocked so I drove down to the house just before Julie arrived. Wow! That must have been a good four hundred yard dash she ran, probably quicker than my Ute would go down a drag strip.

I grabbed the crutches and went up the stairs but could not keep up to her. She was on a mission and I was left in her dust. The door was locked but Julie ran to the window on the left and moved a floor board to reveal a secret stash for the spare key. Julie placed the key in the lock and started to turn it, the empty house echoed like a deep canyon. The massive front doors were about nine foot high and both openings were at least three foot, making this door way wider than a tractor.

I moved forward as Julie yelled, "I'm home!" Then stood still as the sound of her voice cut through the old timber residence.

I watched as the realisation set in that there was no one there.

I felt bad for Julie. I don't know what she was expecting. Maybe her mind was playing tricks on her, being the first time in the house since the murders. Shivers ran up my spine when Julie started talking to her parents, like a full on conversation evolved. I just stood there trying to see what she had seen without any idea.

Then Julie said 'Goodbye and don't worry, I will take good care of the house. Love you all." She blew a kiss into the air. She then turned and kissed me saying, "They have gone."

"Oh, umm… Okay then." I replied taking her into my arms.

It was a very weird thing I just saw, and it is extremely hard to put into words. My straight forward way of life never prepared me for this, but Julie was at ease now and continued into the main entrance.

"It's all good, Mum and Dad have left. They told me to say they were happy to meet you."

I just kept quiet. To be honest, it spooked the daylights out of me.

It took hours for Julie to show me around. Everything was perfect, not even a scratch on the walls. A far cry from our homestead, where the walls were made of mud bricks.

We heard a knock at the door. We made our way down to the front entrance and a lady was standing there.

"Hello Julie, how are you going? So damn great to see you home."

"Beccy!" Julie yelled. "G'day, girlie!" A phrase her father used.

Beccy was a strapper in the stables on the property and had continued to be since the family had gone. Beccy filled us in on the whole thing. I guess you could call her the local newspaper, as she knew it all; and that meant all the town's people as well. Julie had asked if we could stay the night here at Archer Station. I didn't know if this was a good idea. I was still worried about the earlier events of today. I don't have the opportunity to go to movies or that kind of stuff but Merv had told me once of seeing a movie called 'The Poltergeist', where a house was haunted by spirits or some type of shit like that. I kinda like to go up against the things I can see, not the figments in someone's head, but then if Julie has seen something, I guess I am going to need to keep my mind clear because she doesn't normally tell tales. I guess this is the time to trust one another.

"Yes, we will stay." I said, heading out to the veranda which was bigger than our stable.

Beccy headed off to town to get some food. The afternoon was getting on, so staying the night seemed like the best solution. I went down the stairs, it wasn't easy on crutches, but I decided to take a look at the stables where the horses rested. You know, I have seen a lot of things, but never stables that had chandeliers before. This horse area covered a good quarter of an acre. The stables took up half of that.

I must have looked like a kid in a chocolate factory. There were five horses that were top notch thoroughbreds, unlike our worn out nags back at Caplin Station. It puzzled me why Julie left all this behind, but then it hit me… Why the hell she was with me?

They had a lot of those city slicker saddles there, you know, the ones the gay blokes use? I was trying to work out how they rope whilst on them, when another female poked her head out from within the stable.

"CRIKEY!" I said, a saying that old folks said. I think it was something Chips Rafferty said in his old movies. I don't know, but she made my hair stand up taller than a giraffe's head. This place was definitely freaking me out.

"G'day, mate!" She said. "My name is Nat, short for Natalie. Who are you?"

"Jo is my name," I replied. "I am here with Julie."

The girl shrugged her shoulders and said, "Nah! Don't know her. Must be someone from the house."

And then she went back behind the wall shovelling the horse shit into the barrow. The last scoop went in so I grabbed the barrow and asked where they emptied it. She laughed and said it had to go into the cars.

"Oh yeah, sure. You bloody galah! Where does it really go?" I replied with a slight sarcastic grin.

"No, really. It goes to the car garage, it runs the old cars."

"Bullshit!" I said.

"No, horseshit!" she commented with a huge grin.

She led the way to a building at the rear of the house. She opened the door and waved me on in. I stopped like a rabbit in the beam of a headlight. I could not believe my eyes. Inside the shed there were five vintage cars, the type you see in the pictures with the Queen. They must be over eighty years old, it was obviously a collection of some sort. Nat lifted up the back of the car, it looked like a large suitcase. She then told me it had to go in there.

"Okay, you got me." I laughed. "You're a bundle of laughs." I said to her before leaving the shed to find Julie.

I found a door and went in. It was dark and stunk to high heaven. What is this joint? I thought to myself, taking a few steps at a time. Then I saw the pans we use in the outhouse at the homestead. The pans were on some type of mechanism, travelling along to be emptied.

"Bugger," I said as I back peddled to the door. "This is the collection point for the toilets in the house!"

Trying to keep my guts from emptying out, I could not believe this type of thing was used. Too bloody flash for me. Eww!

Eventually, I made my way back in the house. Beccy had returned with the food, along with half of Blackall. It was a big moment for them to have Julie return to the station. It was setting out to be one hell of a party.

Feeling like I needed a shower, I asked a woman where the bathroom was. They just laughed.

"There's five bathrooms here. Which one do you want?" Still laughing.

"There is one in the main bedroom up the staircase," she replied. "Just turn right and head up to the top floor," she pointed.

Surely not, I thought. With my crutches in hand, up I went. Bloody good job I didn't need the dunny! It seemed like ten minutes before I found the bedroom.

Pushing the door open, a chime went off. It was an old alert to let the servants know the head of the household was on the way down for breakfast, I found out later.

Wow! The room was massive. A big round bed filled the centre of the room like a stage. I found the bathroom, it had taps and a shower. It was way more than we ever had back at the homestead. I stripped off and began to run the water. It didn't take long to heat up and scolded me on the ass.

Holy shit! I jumped clear out of the shower. We only had cold water at Caplin Station homestead.

Sorting out the water temperature and soothing my heated up rump, I finished washing. I stepped out into a drying area in front of the screen. There was a towel on the rail so I began to dry myself, looking over to where I took my clothes off. They were nowhere to be seen! No, not there, or there. Where are they?! I thought to myself.

Wrapping the towel around my waist, I headed towards the door. Feeling very uncomfortable, I saw my kit on the table in the hall so I shook the dust off them and put them on. The dust made my skin muddy and it looked worse than before my wash. I felt a hand touch my shoulder, I turned around to find no one. One leg or two, it didn't matter. I shot down those bloody stairs faster than the bluebird when it broke the world land speed record. Standing on the cobblestone driveway, looking back at all the onlookers, I took a moment to catch my breath.

"That's it!" I said. "I'm not going back in that mongrel house. It's haunted."

I could still feel my heart racing. Outside there was a barbecue cooking, the smell of the steaks strangely made my fears fade for a little while but I still had my wits about me.

"Grab a plate," the woman said, as I made my way closer. Julie had already started eating when I found a place to sit.

"Jo!" Julie sang out. "You could have had a wash, you know. You look like you have been rolling around in the stables. Go upstairs and have a wash. I don't want anyone to think you're a hobo!"

68

I'll just eat my food. There was no way I was going back inside. The food was great and everyone was enjoying the evening. A bomb fire had been lit and marshmallows were plentiful. At about eight o'clock, the townsfolk were packing up their equipment. There was all sorts of crap there, from cooking to entertainment. The afternoon had got out of control, almost as big as the Longreach show. I looked at Julie, who was soaking up the attention. It opened up a side of her I never even knew existed. There was no way I could stay here. A bushman sleeps under the stars and I needed to go.

Following the other people to the car park, I was confronted by Gavin, the gentleman I had met the other day. Bloody hell! I used the term gentlemen, I thought to myself. It felt strange. I was glad the others from the homestead were not here to hear me say it, they would never let me live it down.

"I hope everything is okay, Jo!" He said.

"Ah, yes. All good." I replied. "I was just going out to thank very one for turning up."

"Cheers! See ya later," I called out waving to anyone looking in my direction.

Gavin didn't move. He waited until I made my way back to the house. I felt like they were watching my every move. I estimated that probably a hundred people had turned up to see Julie come back to the Archer Station. Life was about to change. I could feel a sense of permanent foundations ending in tonight's shin dig!

I don't know what time it was when the last person left, but it was very late. I was on the veranda with Julie, I had not gone back in the house all evening. The two of us sat alone, looking out at the star filled night. Julie moved closer to me and snuggled in on the cane lounge. It felt like home, but I still ain't going in there, I thought to myself.

"How about you bring some blankets and pillows out Julie? We can camp here on the porch. It is a great night!"

"Good idea," said Julie. "You are such a romantic."

She had no idea how shit scared I was! But it made us bond even closer than ever. I had no idea of the lifestyle she had left to come and shack up with me up at the dirty, dusty old plains of Caplin Station. I don't remember much after that, we drifted off to sleep, listening to the horses echoing as they settled for the night.

CHAPTER SIX

The morning sun from the east lit the house up like a rainbow. The stained glass window in the front doors reflected into my eyes. The glare from the new paint glowed like a diamond on show for the world to see. I couldn't see Julie. She must have gone inside, so I made my way down the stairs and undone my zipper and had a well-deserved leak on the ground. Damn! I needed that, I thought to myself. Looking over my right shoulder up to the railing above, Julie stood shaking her head.

"You will never change, Jo," grinning like a cat that caught a mouse. "Breakfast is nearly ready, come on in and wash your hands first before you do anything else."

"No thanks, I don't want to go in the house. It's haunted!"

"Jo, get in the house now." She stood stomping her feet.

"Don't be foolish, the house is not haunted." She laughed.

"Bullshit!" I said, "Someone took my clothes, then grabbed me on the shoulder yesterday. And I ain't going back in, ever!"

"You whimp!" Julie replied. "It was me, you dumb ringer. I always knew you only had half a brain, but I now know I was being generous. I moved your clothes into the hall. I thought you would have put on the clothes I laid out on the side board. The local clothing store had brought them out for you to wear and I hid in the linen closet and touched you on the shoulder before hiding again, you clown!"

I only had one thing to say. Or maybe two.

"What is a side board? And what the hell is a linen closet?"

The breakfast was on a grand scale. There were three cooks

trying out for Julie's approval, and you guessed it, I am the official taste tester. Julie came and sat beside the table.

"Well, Jo, you had better go back to Caplin Station and let them know we are moving back here now. I am back. I am positive that this is where we need to be. That is, if it's okay by you."

I mean, talk about putting a bloke on the spot. CRIKEY! I still haven't come down from the clouds. I have never worked on a property like this, let alone lived on one.

"So how are the cooks working out?" I asked, trying to avoid answering her question.

"They are not cooks, as you call them Jo, they are chefs." She replied.

If I have never felt out of place before, I did now.

"I will head back to the homestead and let the boys know we are okay. It's been a big couple of days and I was wanting to find out how Noat went at the auction." So I headed for Julie's car when another vehicle entered the driveway. It was a rather large, rounded looking thing. One of those convertible jobs.

A big man got out and put his hand forward and said, "Trevor is the name mate, you must be Jo. I spoke to Julie last night and said I was to bring Mister Archer's car back today. Is the little lady about?"

"Wow Trevor!" I heard Julie yell. "The car looks beautiful. What do you think Jo? This is Daddy's pride and joy. Take it for a spin. Better than that, take it to Caplin Station. It hasn't been driven in ten years. Trevor had the car in his shed, restoring it back to original."

I looked inside and said, "Sorry, I cannot drive it. It has a manual gearbox and I haven't got my artificial leg any more. I will just take your car, Julie."

"Oh sorry, Jo! Yes, take mine. I forgot you need an automatic." She replied.

"Hang on a minute. If you want, I can drive Jo to where he has to go," Trevor interrupted.

"All good, mate. Thanks for the offer, but I have to back to my home out near Jundah."

"Well I can go visit my sister at Jundah," he said. "I haven't seen Trixie for ten years. Besides, I would like to take the car for a good drive. I have only driven it from Blackall to here since I finished it."

"Okay, it's a deal," said Julie. "I will let you two work it out."

I didn't know what to say to Trevor, but I guess the boss has spoken.

"I will just get a cloth to put over the seat," I told him. "Then we should get on our way."

Trevor was a nice bloke. He was one of those laid back types and it was like nothing seemed to worry him. We spoke as he drove along the road back to Blackall.

"What type of car is this, Trevor?" I asked.

"It's a 1937 Cord. One of two in Australia. Mister Archer imported it about eighteen years ago but it was in bad condition, so he asked me to fix it up for him. It's just a shame he is not here to see it."

Thinking to myself, I wondered if Julie heard that if she would say her old man was here looking down on us all. But that's as far as that thought went, I was just happy to get away from that house for a while. It still freaks me out a bit.

We stopped at Trevor's house to get some photos that he wanted to show his sister. I kind of thought his house would be neat but there were old cars everywhere. There was only enough room each side of the drive for one vehicle at a time. The narrow track weaves through a maze of old iron right up to his house. It was very quiet and out of the way, sort of a hidden treasure, or dump, depends on your interpretation of car collecting.

I waited in the car. A couple of scruffy dogs that were barked ferociously drew my attention. They looked like they haven't had a feed for a month. Then I noticed Trevor locking up the shack and heading towards the car with his swag.

"Yep! All set." Trevor said. "It will do me good to get away from this place for a day."

"Well that didn't take long," I replied, only to notice there was a woman and two children hiding in the shed off to the left of the house. "Is that your wife, Trevor?"

"No," he said. "Just some drop kick that had a couple of my kids."

And with that he finished the last of a bottle of beer he had walked out of the house with. He chucked the bottle at the shed with such force that I thought the bloody thing was going to fall down!

"Get back in your hole, you turds!"

My bad temper wanted me to hit him, hard. I don't appreciate anyone talking like that to women and children but I was hesitant, as I needed him to drive the car for a while. I had high regards for Trevor, but now I just want to give him a damned good flogging.

He started the car and drove back out the path we came in on. I sat silently, but I was wound up tighter than a drum of wire. We were almost in Ilfracombe when the next words were spoken.

"Where abouts in Jundah?" I asked Trevor.

"Out by the dry creek flats," he said. "About ten miles west of the pub."

I knew that road and I couldn't help thinking of how damaged this old car would get if he took it out along the flats.

When we finally got into Longreach we stopped and got some fuel. Trevor had gone into the service station to pay and was on his way back to the car. When he approached the car, I had a brilliant idea.

"I have an idea that might be a solution to taking the Cord on those unsealed roads. How about you take my four wheel drive out to your sister's, Trevor? It hasn't been run much since I lost my leg, only Jack and Dave have used it occasionally. Wouldn't want to risk any damage to this beautiful rig."

"Sounds good," Trevor replied.

It was three o'clock when we arrived at the bottom driveway of the homestead. I could see Dave and Noat looking puzzled at what and why such a car was doing out here on the dusty plains. They were fixing the tractor in the shed which hadn't been able to be repaired since long before I ran into it with the Ute.

"Park in the carport," I said pointing the way for Trevor to go. By the time the car stopped I had everyone hanging around. Jack and Merv were at the back of the car, whilst Terry, Noat and Dave were at the front of the car trying to work out what type of vehicle we had arrived in.

I made my way out of the Cord and grabbed my crutches, only to notice my artificial leg sitting on top of the stable fence with two or three bullet holes in it.

"So, I see you found my leg." I said to Noat.

"Oh yeah," he replied. "It was running wild through the paddocks looking for you and scaring the shit out of the cattle, so we shot it."

Shaking my head I said, "You assholes! Nothing is safe with you bastards around. I'm sick of using these bloody crutches though!"

I made my way over and retrieved the damn thing. With a little effort, I slipped it on. Ah! That's better now. I was able to walk again. It may have a few bullet holes and some unsavoury words written on it, but all the same, I am able to walk around unassisted.

With my leg fastened firm, I lead Trevor to where my four wheel drive was parked. It was a far cry from the 1937 Cord in which we arrived in. The keys were still in the ignition, so he got in and it started up right away. He drove over to the fuel tank on the stand next to the tractor shed and stopped, still sitting in the 4WD.

"So who is this bloke and what's the deal with the flash car, Jo!?" asked Dave.

"Well Trevor restored this car for Julie's old man. It has only been on the road for a couple of days so we decided to take it for a run."

"Oh, so you're heading back again?" I heard Noat say.

"Ah! Yes. I will talk to you about that later Noat. I will just get Trevor on his way before it gets too late, he is on his way to see his sister at Jundah."

So with Trevor set off on his trip to Jundah, the sun was on the way down. About half an hour of light left and the boys were packing up for the night. Terry had caught a wild pig yesterday so pork was on the menu. It takes a special technique to prepare a wild boar for eating as the worms and other infestations needed to be cleaned out. I wouldn't know how it is done so that is something the Romanian is good at doing. I sorted out my bed as it hadn't been slept in for a few days, but I had to let the rest of them know that I shall be moving out within the next week but that will be discussed after dinner.

The evening meal was a treat. Terry had worked his magic and turned a tuff carcass into a mouth-watering treat. Not much was said at the table, all heads were down scoffing in the food.

Merv had gone to the Jundah store earlier and had been caught up with a local girl he had his eye on. The rest of us had finished eating by the time he returned. I was in the living room when I addressed Noat with a question of how he faired with the cattle at the auction.

"Well it was a good sale. We will be right for the next six months then those steers we bought not long ago will be ready to go," he said.

I replied by saying, "That's good to hear," and then I cut to the chase with the conversation turning around to where I had been for the past two days.

Merv had finished his food and joined in with a story that he had heard in Jundah earlier. It sorta buggered up me trying to be subtle about leaving.

"Hey Jo! What's this crap I hear about you and Julie being rich and that you are taking over Archer Station?"

Typical of the big shithead throwing me right in the deep end.

"Yes, I am going to move to Archer Station with Julie. To be honest I am not looking forward to it, and thanks to Merv I don't have to explain much else as you know about as much as me now. I definitely am not rich, I am just a bystander heading into a different world and I hope you all can help me with the change as you are my family and blood is thicker than water."

"So, you're telling us that Julie has gone back to her family home and you are going to rebuild it?" Asked Jack.

"Nothing to rebuild, Jack. The whole property is immaculate and it has been kept running by the Blackall community. They have been awaiting Julie's return. I saw it last weekend and Julie didn't know until we went back the other day."

Dave and Noat just got up from their chairs and walked away, not saying a word. Terry, Jack and Merv came over and congratulated me and told me to give the boys a bit of time to take it in as Noat had just signed a contract with Dalgety which relied on the crew expanding the property workload. After a few rums with Jack, I hit the sack for the night.

As always, everyone was up at the break of dawn. I went down to the stables to prepare the horses for the day's work when Noat yelled out from the veranda.

"Leave those horses alone, Jo! You don't work here anymore."

"What the hell are you talking about, Noat?" I replied.

"Grab your gear and piss off! You're not a part of this crew anymore, you scum."

And with that I made my way towards the house to confront him.

"Where do you get off with that garbage?" I said. "I haven't made my mind up yet but you're going the right way about making it for me."

"Oh yeah, sure mister big shot. As if you would rather stay here than live with little miss smarty pants. That whore has got you wrapped around her little finger, you loser. You're just Julie's little bitch!"

That was it. I ran towards the stairs and took them three at a time. With my fist clasped as tight as a vice, I raised it to swipe at Noat. When all of a sudden I was grabbed and sent to the floor.

"What the bloody hell did you do that for Merv, you prick! I thought we were mates."

"We are," he replied. "But that is not the way to fix this problem. Come on, I will give you a hand to collect your belongings."

Rubbing the back of my head, I lifted myself from the deck and darted Noat a filthy look.

It took most of the morning to load the car with everything. I had told Trevor that I would be at Caplin for a few days so he wasn't going to return anytime soon.

So now I have my prosthesis I am hoping I can drive the old car. Jack, Dave, Merv and Terry gathered around to send me off but Noat was nowhere to be seen. A lifetime of friendship turned into a disappointing end.

With the engine idling, I looked at the front of the house to see if Noat would appear but nothing. I selected the reverse gear and backed out from the carport and lined myself up for the exit along the driveway. Into first gear, I released the clutch, stalling the motor in what could only be explained by the term 'jumping like a kangaroo'. It was more difficult to manoeuvre than I had anticipated.

Off I went again. The second attempt was much better. I got into the rhythm of it. By the time I got halfway down the drive, I looked back and waved. I still did not locate Noat. As much as he pissed me off last night, I still consider him like a brother. I felt sadness in my heart, but to be in control of this beautiful machine, I felt like a king.

Arriving at Longreach, I pulled into the service station to get a drink. The warm summer air had dried my lips.

Opening the door to the car, I struggled to get out. My artificial leg made the task very awkward and I almost ended up on my ass. Eventually I managed to vacate with some dignity. The car had attracted a rather big crowd by the time I returned from inside. Almost twenty people, including the local newspaper reporter Tanya Donnelly, who was the best around these woods.

"Hello Jo," Tanya said as I went to open the door. "I am wondering how you came about the late Mister Archer's Cord, and I was wondering if you can tell me anything about the vehicle?"

"The car belongs to my fiancé, Julie Archer," I replied.

"As far as knowing anything about the car, I wouldn't be able to comment."

I clambered back into the Cord, not responding to anyone who were around. Readjusting myself to a suitable driving position, I began the drive to Blackall.

It was late afternoon before I arrived back at Archer Station. I entered the property slowly. It was an overwhelming emotion that took hold, knowing that from now on this will be my home. I drove to the end of the driveway and turned around the circular entry. Julie came from within the house and made her way down the stairs to greet me with arms wide open and kissing me wildly. Is this home or is this heaven?

CHAPTER SEVEN

The morning had arrived. This the first day Julie and I adjust to our new environment. I woke up at four and headed out to the yards to check over the livestock. It really looked amazing. The white post and rail fences enclosed a well-bred array of beef. I entered the stables and began searching for a suitable horse that I could use for the chores. My first choice was a big thoroughbred by the name of Radish. His size and temperament was worth closer inspection.

Nat, the stable hand, called me to an enclosure to a horse nick named Stan. A name which originated from his breed. The standard breed is not known for its stock work attributes so it would not be my choice of steed. I took the horse into the arena to see what he had to offer. Saddled up, the standard bred stood firm as I raised myself onto the stallion. It is the first time I have attempted to ride an unfamiliar horse since I lost my leg.

Kicking the spurs into the underside of the girth, I took hold as he lifted high and threw himself into a frenzy. Using all my knowledge and brute strength, I withered away his stubborn streak. After about thirty minutes I had control and I was exhausted. I got the strapper to set out some barrels to see how fast this boy will go. With the first cut I almost lost my balance, but the second, he just trimmed the objects in a record breaking time.

"Okay," I said. "After about two hours testing the skills, it seems like Stan has come through with the goods."

The use of my bullet-ridden artificial leg was a godsend. It gave me the confidence to do what I do best. Being a ringer has never been a perfect life. I found I could not stay in one place too long, so getting back in the saddle gave me a positive insight into the future. Or so I thought.

Walking the horse back to remove the gear, I noticed Julie had come down to see what I was doing and did not look at all happy.

"So you having fun playing around with the hired help, Jo?" Julie shouted.

"That's a bit rude," I said. This was my first lesson on not to talk back to Julie.

She stormed off into the house, muttering some words that even I had never used in my life and that wasn't many, I tell you.

"Are you okay with Stan? I asked Nat. "I had better go in and sort this out."

Inside, Julie was sitting, stomping her foot on the floor like an angry bull preparing to charge.

"So you would rather be in the stables with the tart than in bed beside me? Is that it, Jo?"

"Hang on a minute," I said. "The girl was just helping me with the horse, nothing more. Get over it. I have to go back to work."

With that, I headed out the door towards the stables.

"You don't have to do anything here, Jo. Just sit and have a coffee or a beer!" Julie exclaimed.

It stopped me in my tracks. I am a ringer, a drover and a planner. My life is lived by hands on performance. Nat had just tethered the horse. It was still saddled when I got back to the stables. I just untied him and went out into the yards. A group of men were rounding the herd into the shutes, separating the cattle for branding. I watched as they went about their business. It was like a precision display of cutting that one can only learn by years of experience. I wanted to join in but I had to take off for a while to clear my head. Handling this type of confinement is playing havoc causing a lack of independence.

A lot of changes have been brought about recently. I lose my leg, and now I feel as though my freedom has been taken away. As much as I love Julie, I cannot just sit back and neglect everything I know.

The day was a little bit overcast. With the sun breaking through the clouds, it lit up the dust rising as the cattle made their way through the yards. My hat tipped to reflect the glare, I headed to the outer fence line of the property.

About a mile into the ride I came across a small river. Not a creek, but a wide body of strong flowing water. It was what every property owner dreamed of. I turned south and followed the banks along. It travelled for miles, until the stream seem to disappear into the ground.

It is an amazing sight that I could not explain. From there on, I rode a bit more. My mind wandering through ideas, filled with using the water for all sorts of enterprising marketing ideas. Like I said, I am a planner. Once I get the bug, there's no stopping my ingenuity.

I made my way back to the property. The yards were cleared out, the branding had been done and the cattle were set in the green pastures to replenish. I entered the stables feeling better about being here.

I left Nat to look after Stan and went inside for the evening. Julie come out to the rear landing with a smile that out done the sunset. She didn't say a word, but I went into the house where Julie came down to meet me.

"I am sorry," I said to her. "I have been so self-centred and haven't given much thought to your return to the property. I hope you will forgive me."

We went back to the landing and watched the sun as it was dissolved by the land for the night. Our embrace held firm as we kissed looking into each other's eyes. You don't need words to describe this, just a trust in true love.

After regaining the bond that Julie and I have, we decided to wind down for the evening. I woke up at four in the morning and just turned over and gave my girl a cuddle. As much as I wanted to stay, my years on the land drew me to get up and start the new day. I never went down stairs just went out to the rear veranda and looked upon this great spread for today. I did feel a hand on my shoulder, conformation from Julie's late father, I suppose. I really think I can make a go of this place. My projection of how the property needs to be run made me write down some notes to be used at a later date. I contacted the house lady, Vanessa, and suggested I meet all those who work here.

Julie woke up and made her way down to the front of the house where I was making myself known to everyone. It was not as daunting as I had anticipated and I was made to feel welcome. I felt Julie's encouraging vibe as confirmation of my decision to take the reins and bring this property to a new level. It was my chance to be in control. I recognised Billy Bull, an indigenous bloke that helped us out at Caplin from time to time. A damned good black tracker who knew everything about these areas. I took him to one side and asked what he knew about the water that went into the ground.

"That would be black fella land," he said. "It was taken from us years ago. It is sacred, protected by spirits of my ancestors, boss!"

It puzzled me why the land was taken from the aboriginals. Billy also told me that it was formed by an underground stream being exposed. When the spirits were angry, the land fell in. When tribes were participating in tribal conflict, the gods were unhappy and swallowed the warriors.

Now, I don't know much about their beliefs, but it is something I will have to make myself aware of as I need the native families in the area to support my plans to channel the water into the nearby paddocks in an attempt to grow crops. It was a way out idea, but where there's water, there is hope.

The day was pretty much a time for me to explore the yards and familiarise how it was setup. A lot of things were impractical, and there was a lot of double handling.

I started to incorporate some of my perspectives. Most of the workers were willing to adjust, but five of them wouldn't hear of the changes and just walked off. This being in charge business is going to take some time to engineer.

Julie called me to the house. This was done with a triangle device that rang out as it was hit by a steel bar. It was very old fashioned, but I guess it worked. Afternoon coffee break, just what I need. Mmm! Freshly made fruit biscuits. The smell made my mouth water. I took a sip of my cuppa when a car came in the driveway. It was Allan from the Dalgety store at Longreach. I hadn't seen him since I took his Ute to get home from the hospital earlier this year.

"G'day, Jo." He said as he got out of the car. "I didn't expect to see you here."

"I'm running the place now, Al. Julie and I are together, and this is where we live."

Julie just smiled and said, "Well you have changed your tune, Jo." She paused momentarily. "Anyway, what brings you out here Allan?"

"Just doing the rounds of the area and looking for new clients. Is there anything I can do to be of assistance, Jo?"

We left Julie to what it was she was doing in the garden and I took Allan for a tour of the property.

"Very impressive, I must say, Jo!" He said.

Our walk turned into a discussion about growing crops and he agreed there is a shortage of good produce in the shire.

"What if I told you I can get access to as much water as I need?"

He just laughed and said I was full of shit, I never replied just kept what he said to myself and told him to come back next week when I worked out what I needed.

I went into the library where I met some of the locals on my first trip out to Blackall. I wanted to find out more on farming and if the soil was suitable. I had brought a few samples with me hoping that someone could help.

Ernie Anderson, a small framed man, said as he put his hand forward, "I hear you have taken over the Archer Station?"

"Yeah, that's right," I replied.

"Good," he said. "You look like you know what you're doing."

Well if that was the case, then he knows more than me. I was out of my depth.

"I need to know how to get water from four miles away," I said. "Do you know who can fill me in on how to do that?"

Well it turned out that Ernie is a surveyor for the council. His knowledge of the land above and below, makes him the best person to be talking to about this. It turns out that the land around here is very rich in nutrients and if it was closer to the water it would be perfect for growing.

He took me to the council office and met with the local mayor. It seems that my idea of farming had already been on Mister Archer's mind before his death. I was shown paperwork and planning for a pumping station built at the site I had visited last week. It appears that the water is fed by the Thompson River outside of Longreach, and Archer and the council were joining forces in a joint partnership to pipe water into the town. Now, I think I know why the Archer property meant so much to the township.

Things were going well. We have been at Archer Station for four months now. The property is changing and money is rolling in, making it easier to afford equipment that we need. The council have given me a loan of a backhoe and drilling gear and negotiations are still on the table about water distribution. Julie has taken on the task of running the household, as Vanessa, the house lady, had to leave and look after her ill mother. The property has dwellings for the employees, and it has taken time to make them liveable again so most of the staff live onsite now. I went out on a ride with three other men to check the fences. This is something critical, as the downing of a fence not only counts for a loss of cattle, but also the risk of other animals invading the grazing land.

Back at the stables, it was late morning and everything was very quiet. I couldn't see many workers out and about so it had a sense of no good about it. I went around the front of the house to see what was going on when, "SURPRISE!"

"What the f!" I yelled as balloons and banners covered the veranda.

"Happy birthday Jo!" They all cried out.

"Come on up, you old bugger!" I heard from above.

I have never had a chance to celebrate my birthday before. When I was four, my parents sent me to a home and took off, never to be seen again. I had no idea why, but since that day, I was on my own. Right up until Noat's old man took me in all those years ago. To tell you the truth, I don't know what date my birthday is. I mixed in and took the congratulation kisses and hugs which I thought was only polite. I had never seen so many people in the same place before. I have always signed my name as Joseph Bounty. I don't know my real name, and it is something I had never thought about. But after talking to a few people I realised I may have to find out in order to marry Julie. I guess that can wait for another day for now, it is time to enjoy the festivities.

"Yahoo!" I yelled as more and more people arrived.

Times were different for sure. I got presents worth more than my old Ute, which reminds me, Trevor had never returned it from his trip to Jundah. I got four watches and I have never found the need to keep an eye on time.

What gets done, gets done, I say. It was a great day that went late into the night. Only a few stragglers stayed until the next morning. I had already been up for hours checking the cattle before the others decided to rear their sorry heads. I headed to see Julie, who was in the main bedroom with three other young ladies on the bed as well. I think a reunion between old friends had flourished again for Julie. I tried to wake her but she was out to it. Looking at my arm, I had three watches on it. I guess one of them must be on the right time, I thought. Approximately nine o'clock, so I decided to head into town and pursue my identity. Entering the town hall, I asked a lady behind the counter if she knew how I find out who I am.

"Wow! It must have been a big night," she said. "Your name is Jo, silly."

"I know that, but I want to find my real name. How do I do that?"

"It would be on your birth certificate," she said.

"And what's that?" I replied, confused beyond belief.

"Are you for real, Jo? You actually don't know who you are?"

I spent the morning talking to different people in the building, working out how to find out who I was. The mayor got involved and it amazed me how many phones they have in these joints. Old Maureen would have a heart attack connecting all these hook ups, I thought to myself.

"Do you know when you were born, Jo?"

"Sorry. I don't have a clue."

Half the council and the local police went on mission to find who

I was. It may be strange, but I lived all my life in the bush and had no idea who or where I came from.

"Do you know how old you are?"

"Pass," I said.

"Do you know where you were born?"

"Pass," I said again.

Almost five hours passed. I knew that because I have been watching the watches on my arm.

"I found it!" A girl in the other office yelled out. "I know who you are!"

It turns out, Noat's old man and his ex-wife had adopted me when I was five. Which meant Noat was somehow my brother for real. It turns out my name is Philip Joseph Salvadoro.

"Hey, I'm a bloody wog!" I cried out.

And I am thirty three years of age and my birthday is a month away. I felt faint, as my life had been without a connection with the outside world.

"How can you be sure?" I asked.

"Well, you were born in a Victorian town called Tatura.

I have asked them to send all the paperwork up here as soon as they can but it might take two months."

"So what do I do now?" I said to the mayor.

"Well we will give you a citizenship form and I will approve it and the Deputy Sergeant will co-sign the form and the process will begin. Welcome, Philip!" He said.

I shook my head and thought to myself how I was going to tell Julie.

CHAPTER EIGHT

It has taken a while to come to terms with my new identity. People still call me Jo, but it seems that everything I have done in my life is now dissolved. Talk about a new start. Well you cannot get better than this. I am hoping to go back to Caplin later on this week to catch up with Noat as I need to see his father. I have only ever known him as Uncle Pete, not aware that he was my adopted father.

Council alerted us that the paperwork had come through, so Julie took me to the court house where they stamped my birth certificate and the local copper gave me a license. It's a long story, but I got my other one drinking piss at Jundah, but no one will ever know.

Julie and I set out to Caplin Station. It was a long drive, but full of admiration for this beautiful land. My drive seemed like a new path into the future and I couldn't wait to tell the boys.

We drove into the driveway. The door to the house was off the hinges and rubbish all about it. It kinda resembled a ghost town. Cautiously, I got out near the carport and started to look around. There was no livestock or anyone about. I could not understand what had happened since I left. It was no use hanging around here.

"Let's go into Jundah and see if they can fill us in," I said to Julie who had locked herself in the car.

Arriving at the sale yards, I came across Barry, an old friend. I asked him if he knew anything about Caplin Station and where Noat and the boys are.

"Didn't you hear, Jo? Terry the Romanian shot himself at those old cottages at the back of the land, Jack and Dave took off for some unknown reason and left Noat to deal with it all on his own. And whilst the coppers investigated Terry's death, they found another body that had been buried not far from where Terry was found, so Noat was arrested and his court case is being held in Charleville next week. So the place has been deserted. Dalgety's came and moved the cattle, as Noat's contract was cancelled."

I felt sick knowing that Noat had been accused of Casper Norton's murder. I was caught between my life now and my previous time where things were spent doing what we had to do. Now it has come back to bite us on the ass.

Julie and I decided to make our way back to Longreach in search of Noat's location. We went to the cop shop and talked to the Constable at the front desk. He informed us that Noat was being held at the cells here in Longreach itself. I asked if we could see him, but the officer came back a short time later, stating that Noat had told him to tell me to go, and that he was in no mood for talking with me. As Julie was aware of what happened to Casper Norton, she was just as oblivious to the where abouts of his body, as I was.

We went to the pub for some lunch, and after speaking to a few locals, I was told that Terry had been a Romanian soldier and was in Australia illegally and when he was informed he had to return to his own country, he couldn't handle it and topped himself. I mean, I never thought Terry would have done something like that, but I didn't know the life he had before he came to Caplin ten years ago. Allan from Dalgety was also at the pub. We chatted for a while. It is only today that he too found out about the events unfolding at Caplin.

Julie spoke to me a bit later and said, "Don't you dare! I know you, Jo, and you are feeling guilty about Noat taking the fall for Casper. But leave it to the courts. All we can do is help by getting one of Daddy's old lawyers to fight the charges."

Feeling down, I agreed.

All this over a mongrel that deserved to die for what he did to the Archer family. Unable to talk to Noat, we headed back to Blackall. On the way, we stopped at Toby Jamieson's place. He had a lot of old machinery in his yard and I wanted a pump to siphon some water out of the stream. I found an old belt driven pump that I knew I could get to run off the old tractor, so I bought it and hit the road again. It was about 11:30 at night when we made it back to Archer Station. All was quiet so we just had coffee and cake, then went off to bed.

I was unable to sleep. I tossed and turned throughout the night, thinking about Noat and how I could help but without taking the whole blame myself, there wasn't much I could do. Julie was right, let the courts handle it.

I woke up more tired than I had gone to bed. Julie was still sleeping like a log.

So much has happened and so many changes going on in my life. The phone rang and I answered it. Expecting Maureen to be connecting someone, but the phones here are updated to what they call STD (whatever that is). Anyway, the phone call was from Steve, the area salesman, for Elders, a farming identity, around these areas. He had heard about my idea of planting crops on Archer Station and Elders have offered funds to build the pumping station, and with that verbal conversation the deal was set. My instincts had led me to consider a cattle drive along some other folk in the area. As much as water was great to have, to start crops, grazing land was getting scarce. It only takes a few weeks with this type of heat to dry the countryside out. So we are taking the herds towards Augathella to feed for a couple of months, which will also clear the property so pipe laying can commence.

It had been a long time since I had to use my droving skills. My ringer days were slowly fading, but I had been nominated to lead the drive down south. I hope it a goes to plan, as my reputation depends on this. I rigged the new boy, Stan the standard breed horse, onto the buggy.

I had spent a day or two training him to pull the cart. It is one thing to get a rider on their backs, but hitching a buggy behind them takes work. The first workout was fine, then I left him to just drag the buggy as I walked beside him. That was fine too, until I lost my footing and let go of the reins. Well, I never knew the old buggy could go so fast or bounce so high. Before long, it was out of sight. Billy Bull the tracker took off after him and returned a short time later with horse and buggy intact.

"Good enough," I said. "He will do fine."

Billy just laughed and commented, "Bloody white blokes."

"Piss off, you black bastard!" I replied, as putting shit on each other was the way we supported each other out these parts.

Although my years as a ringer had its advantages, droving is a bit more full on. To foresee the weather and source routes to keep the animals safe had to be taken into account. I had some experience riding alongside Terry when Caplin Station was at its best, but now I have to try and pick a handful of men to ride with me and that won't be easy only having known the crew at Archer for a few months. Back at the stables, Nat the strapper, who had a knack of caring for horses, was talking to a big steed by the name of Radish. I could have sworn he was listening to every word she spoke. Nat came over to me and said, "I hear you're moving cattle down to Augathella, Jo, Philip, or whatever your name is now!" She laughed.

"Jo is fine, Nat," I said.

"Any chance I can come along?" She asked.

A woman amongst the drovers? I am not sure about that out here, but it was not heard of back where I'm from.

"No," I replied. "Ladies don't work cattle."

My god, if I never get to see the devil, I think I seen the next best thing. Her eyes turned into a fury of emotions, and her nostrils flared wide like a rampaging bull. Throwing the horse gear she had in her hand to the ground, Nat tore out of the stables faster than a rock in a landslide. I stood silent for a moment as I turned around to see Billy was sitting on a bale of hay, his head lowered to disguise his grin.

"You tell her, boss. No womens on the ride, hey?"

I looked for a while to find the strapper, but she was nowhere to be seen. I have not had much contact with girls in my working life, nor in my social life either, so my manners needed a bit of polishing. It was then I saw a horse go full pelt towards the yard fence, with a rider upon its back. The gates were five foot high and there wasn't a chance the horse would stop in time. Not even a flinch from rider or horse, not a step was altered, and in full stride the gate was no challenge for this man and his beast. Throughout the yards and down the fence line, the rider came back again. The silhouette of a stockman, confident and brawn once again, the gate disappeared under the shadow of the stockman and his steed. Out of sight in no time flat. I stood amazed. I have but praise for this rider. Moments later, the horse came back in view. I knew I had to get this bloke in my crew. I looked around and could see the men watching in disbelief. I knew then I had to find a way to encourage this man to my team.

The horse had sweat running down its side and the rider was still refreshed. They came nearer to the stables and I watched as all jaws dropped as the pretty little stable hand tilted her hat.

"Farewell boys! I'm leaving. And Mister Jo, shove your job up your arse!"

Spurs deep into the skin, the steed and rider mounted the mound of dirt and reared high into the air like the Lone Ranger and took off leaving everyone standing in awe!

"I think she took that okay, boss." Billy said, with his hat pulled down over his nose. "Bloody good rider, you reckon, boss?"

I just walked away. It was my first, but probably not my last time, I will take someone for granted.

"Okay, the show's over. Get back to work!" I yelled, as my dignity hit a new low.

It took two days to find a new strapper, but none of the animals were ever the same. Always unsettled and restless, as if they were fretting.

Julie was happy that the strapper had gone. I guess I did check her out a bit more than I should, but I know one thing for sure: I would rather work with cattle, than women!

It is only a week away from the start of the cattle drive, so I have picked two of my best men and two stable boys for the ride. They were all green, but that will soon change. I had made arrangements for the horses and the men to be transported back at the end of the ride to save downtime, which will be better spent back at Archer Station. A week seemed like a couple of days. The morning has come to begin our journey. Eight hundred head of cattle filled our yards, four hundred and fifty were ours, the rest were from two other stations close by, as these drives don't happen very often these days due to big trucks transporting large amounts across the outback, driving them on the land did not only feed them as they went, but also made for better quality stock. The exercising helped with the health of the beast and it was a cheaper alternative to move such a large herd.

Well talk about a send-off! Most of Blackall and surrounding areas had turned out to see us off. Bloody reporters were chasing us amongst the cattle. Last thing we wanted was them stirred up as we headed out. Billy had his two dogs, and Bluey May had brought along his dog, Reno. I put the two stable boys, Tony and Ray, in the buggy with the supplies. They will head out after us to stay out of harm's way and also stop the two relief horses tied to the back of the buggy from going hypo when the cattle are on the move.

It had taken a lot of planning. Billy had sourced a path down to Augathella over the past two months.

Everybody is aware we will be coming down and they have set dates to have the fences down for the cattle to pass through, so to not inconvenience them too much.

The timing is critical as a schedule is in place that we have to work by. We cannot get held up with this size herd, and only a few men. It is easier to manage our travelling group, than trying to hold them in one place. It wasn't hard to hear the hundreds of people cheer as we exited the yards. I must admit, I don't think we have a chance of making it far, but the cattle need to get to better pastures.

With only two men on the outside flanks and myself guarding the rear, the dogs are our only hope of keeping control. The dust was tremendous, our spit felt like sand as we made it to the first gully ten miles away. In order to move the cattle to the other side, we had to prevent any of them going astray into the weathered path. Billy took the sights of the gully whilst Bluey directed them onto the paddock over the embankment. Reno, Bluey May's dog, received a big hit as a large Brahman bull lashed out with his back legs, sending Reno into the air.

There is one thing about these Australian cattle dogs, they are tough little buggers. Limping on three legs, he put the beast back in its place. It has taken most of the day to get twelve miles into the ride. The two boys had caught up. It was great to see the buggy, my guts was rumbling from hunger. I called out to Billy and Bluey to halt, as we will set up camp in the low lying land.

The herd settled down. It was the first night and no one can tell how it was going to play out. Ray tried to light a fire with a lighter with no luck. So Billy Bull took over with just a couple of twigs and some dried up mully weed. He had smoke, and like they say, where there's smoke, there's fire. Eventually a flame appeared and we were set. Gathering wood was easy as there is so much dry timber about. Billy had found some mushrooms and with the cans of beans, our gourmet dinner was served. It had been an exhausting day, so I took first watch over the herd whilst the others rested. The moon light was almost like a security light over the cattle and made it easy to locate the strays.

Holding a stick upright on the ground, I could tell it was midnight. I woke Bluey up and he took over the watch. The morning light was very faint, the wind was blowing in a southerly direction which made for a great day. The cattle were very still as the rest of us woke up and began to stir. It was a good start to the ride. Billy broke thirty or so steers from the pack. These were to be our leaders, the others soon followed and we were on our way.

The sun breaking over this beautiful land was sight only seen in the Australian outback. There had been a slight drizzle of rain two days ago, just enough for the wild flowers to raise above the grass. I am not much of a romantic, nor was this the time to be soft, but the splendid colour of yellow and purple flowers set a picturesque canvas for our cattle drive. Everything had been going great, I think somehow the herd knew they were headed for better grazing and were happy to comply. The morning had been without incident, the boys were in good spirits, Bluey had taken the lead following a path to the trees ahead, Billy was on the left flank, whilst young Ray had saddled up and trimmed the right hand off the group, trying his best to learn as he went.

It was a bit after midday when we stopped for a feed. We cannot stay too long as we have to get past the break before nightfall to have any chance of detaining the herd for the evening. Billy was our only way of heating the water, cooking our meals and doing the dishes, so it was the most important bit of equipment in the buggy, and guess what? It somehow had fallen out from the storage department and most likely bounced out, but there was no doubt the lack of experience in the bush from the two young blokes had played a part in its disappearance. The damper we had made last night became a treat as we ate cold baked beans for lunch.

"Hello there strangers," voices rang out from the trees ahead.

It was Jack and Dave, the Taylor brothers.

"Well aren't you two a sight for sore eyes?" I replied.

"Heard you were heading out, so we thought we would see if you wanted a hand," Dave called out.

I just nodded my head and waved them in. It was good to catch up for I had a few questions that needed sorting out, but that can wait for now. We have to get a move on as the herd has to get past the ridge before we set down for the night. It will save a lot of time in morning as flat plains will make work easier to start the days muster.

Jack, as always, took the young blokes by his side and told them of yarns of long ago which is quite ironic, as he is the youngest of us all by at least ten years.

Along the ride, Bluey had noticed that there was a fence up ahead that has blocked our path. It is not what we need today, of all days. The next two hours crossing the ridge would be hard and demanding, and it is just as well that Jack and Dave turned up when they did. Going ahead snipping the wire and running it outwards gave the herd a path to get through. Jack followed us towards the ridge, whilst Dave and Ray tended to the re-tensioning of the fence. Jack may be a penny short of a quid but he has no fear when it comes to sorting out the steers.

About ten of them had ventured off and when Jack tried to turn them back in, he came of his steed and two bulls decided to challenge him. Well it was like a bloody turtle trying to catch a lizard. Eventually the cattle gave up and went back into the herd, they just assumed Jack was as crazy as we had figured. Dave and Ray had caught up with us again by now.

The travel through the ridge was jagged and uneven. Not only do we have to get the cattle through safely, but the wellbeing of the horses needed to be considered as well. No vets out here, so a lame horse will need to be put down. But with good horsemanship, it will be okay.

If a plan was ever going to work well, then it did today. The union of man, steed and beast bonded as one. It was the best ridge crossing I have ever experienced.

"Well done everyone. We will set up camp by that stream. Jack, you take Ray and the other young bloke out about three miles and check what we have ahead for the morning whilst it's still light," I said to him.

Off they went while the rest of is made camp and boxed in the herd.

The next few days we cruised along with very little problems. Billy Bull went ahead scouting for fresh paddocks to feed the herd as the past days had been baron and dry. Water and feed is essential for the cattle drive and its success. With our billy gone and Jack and Dave having some of their own, it made cooking easier.

Tony, one of the young lads, has fallen ill, so with little medical supplies, a mixture of roots and berries that Billy Bull had prepared should help him. These aboriginal remedies have more to offer than we white folk give them credit for.

I sat by the fire which had been kept going over night. Jack and Dave started to tell me what happened at Caplin Station the day

Terry decided to do himself in.

Apparently his parents and sisters had been killed in an ambush over in his country and when the authorities found him to notify what had happened, it turned out he was an illegal immigrant and they requested that he handed himself in for deportation as soon as possible. No one is sure about his reasons for doing what he did, but I guess he had his reasons not to return to Romania. Terry had taken off for a few days when the police came looking for him. Knowing that he was an experienced bushman, they brought black trackers with them in case he had decided to go bush. Two days later, Noat was checking the fence line when a policeman came upon Terry's body. It was a quick conclusion that he had shot himself, but not far away the officers and black trackers found Casper Norton's remains and took Noat in for questioning. Noat refused to talk to anyone. Dave and Jack were thinking they would release Noat, but it never happened.

The coppers want to nail Noat for the murder. It turns out that there was nothing they could do. Jack and Dave tried to confess, but the police just accused them of making up a cover story to get Noat out of the lock up.

So the boys decided to lay low for a while. Caplin Station was under police guard whilst the investigations were taking place, meanwhile Dalgety's pulled the contract. There was no use hanging about, so Jack and Dave moved on, looking for work elsewhere.

It was only one more day's ride into Augathella. Billy Bull had returned about four days ago and the herd had been feeding on good grazing land for the past day. We settled in for the night. It is always a tradition to have a few drinks and relax the night before we ended the cattle drive.

"I don't know if that's true, but a bloody good drink would go down well, so let's get into it!" I said.

I think the first two bottles just washed the dust out of our gums after swallowing two week's worth of soil. The taste finally hit the spot. It was early morning when we emptied the last of the grog, and no one was in the mood for sleep. The adrenalin was thriving as the team gathered themselves for the run into town. I must say, watching the herd go into the paddocks of green lustrous feed was a feeling of achievement and with the town folk welcoming us on our arrival, the boys were on a high.

Jack was acting like a cross between Charles Bronson and Gregory Peck. His ten seconds of fame has gone to his head since the cameras focused on him.

It was a grand end to our ride. The cattle were now settled into the open pastures of Augathella. All the horses and gear have been loaded on the trucks, ready for transporting back to Archer Station. Julie had driven a Rolls Royce from her father's collection down to meet up with us. It has been a hell of a ride, but it gave us all a feeling of satisfaction knowing that we achieved a trek worthy of our ancestors.

I don't know whether I am getting soft in my old age but my ass was sore from riding. The idea of a cosy drive on soft leather seats back to our property had definitely got my vote. We stayed at the Augathella property overnight and it gave myself and Julie some intimate time together.

I just could not keep my hands off her and it soon turned into a night of lust. Well the cattle drive had come to a close, and the money it saved bringing them down is a bonus. The herd will stay there and will be transported to Roma for auction in a month's time. The prices are better at the Roma auctions, so we hope to make a big profit. Julie sorted out the last of the equipment as I talked the residents of the property, arranging the fees for the access to the grazing land. It was a pleasant drive as we headed back to Archer Station. The Rolls Royce was automatic, so I was able to take over from time to time. Having only ever seen one or two of these cars in my life, I never thought I would ever be behind the wheel of one.

Julie decided that we would stop for the night in Blackall. The pub was a good spot for a meal and accommodation. When we arrived at the hotel, Merv followed us into the carpark. His big grin said it all. He was like a big kid, skipping around the Rolls and checking over every detail.

"It's bloody good to see you two," Merv said as we gathered our suitcases and headed into the reception area.

"Yes, it has been a while, Merv," I replied. "You should head out to Archer Station one day and have a look around."

I shook Merv's hand and he headed back out to his van to continue his run.

Julie had been talking to Annette, the girl behind the counter, who gave her the key to our room.

"Don't you remember me, Jo?" Another lady on reception called out.

Oh shit! I thought to myself. It was the wife of the police officer I had an affair with a number of years ago. I think her name was Christine.

"Umm… Hi." I replied. "Yes, I remember you. Christine, isn't it?"

"No! It's Anita."

She sent me an evil eye that sliced right through me and she huffed off down the stairs. I just shrugged my shoulders and stood beside Julie before heading to the room.

We sat out on the balcony outside our room. It over looked the Main Street. It was a quiet night, and most of the locals had started to head off home. The moonlight shone, highlighting the old building, as lovely as it was, we decided headed off to bed for the night.

It was four in the morning when I woke Julie up and told her I wanted to get an early start. We had our complimentary breakfast and headed out of town. It takes about thirty five minutes to get to the Archer Station homestead from Blackall. By the time we got home, the workers had already started for the day.

Arriving back at Archer Station, I noticed a caravan parked by the house. I had no idea whose it was, or what it was doing there. Ray, one of the stable hands that went along on the ride, opened the door to the garage and I drove inside.

We got out of the car and I turned towards the door when Jack popped up right in front of me, with Dave a few feet away.

"Welcome back, Jo. Where have you been? We have been waiting for you."

"Julie and I had just decided to take our time coming back," I replied. "So why are you here?"

"We are here to help, Jo. Remember? You gave us a job when we were on the ride."

"Oh? When was that?" I asked.

"The night before the ride ended," Dave's voice picked up from around the corner.

Well I guess that explains the caravan, I thought to myself.

"Well I don't remember that," I said. "But I guess while you are here, you can help out for a while before you go back to Caplin Station."

Jack and Dave looked at each other and both said, "We ain't going back to Caplin!"

"Noat won't be coming back for a while and last we heard, Dalgety's were trying to take Noat to court for breach of contract." Jack concluded the sentence.

That was not something I was expecting to hear, but it took me by surprise. I know Noat and I had a falling out, but Caplin was

104

a big part of my past and I knew I couldn't do anything about it. But still, it saddened me.

Jack and Dave fitted in well with the rest of the crew. Their experience set them apart from the green horns I had amongst the other members. I made Jack the foreman. It didn't sit well with his older brother, Dave, but I considered who was the best man for the job and over the past few days, Jack had proven he had grown up and matured enough to take control. Allan from Dalgety's had arrived and the work had begun on the pipeline. I jumped in the four wheel drive and headed out to the pump site.

"Oh my god!" I blurted out as the whole area had been excavated. Not a skerrick of grass to be seen. Steve from Elders was supervising the project. His ideas were very optimistic and he wasted no time getting started. Allan and I walked into the site office to talk to Steve but when we entered the building Steve was in a meeting with four men in suits and kindly asked us if we could wait outside until the meeting had finished. Well, it's Julie's land. I should be able to go where ever I wanted and when I wanted, but I obliged by going back outside.

Whilst Allan and I waited, I began to ask him if he knew anything about Dalgety's attempting to take control of Caplin Station. Allan began to tell me all about the breach of contract order that Dalgety's had over Caplin.

Apparently with Noat's lack of education, he signed the property over to Dalgety's as collateral against the contract and now they have served him with an eviction notice. It just sounded way over my head so I just let it be. Steve was seeing the last of his visitors off when we went back to the office. He introduced the gentleman to me as Dave, a federal member for North Queensland. I shook his hand and he got into his vehicle and headed for Longreach. Steve told me that they had just approved a payment schedule for the state to cover the cost of the pumping station, so the plans are now being revised on a bigger scale.

"Does that mean more machinery and a heavier traffic flow?" I asked.

"Yes, it definitely will, Jo. But you will be paid well for the inconvenience," Steve smiled. "As a matter of fact, here is a cheque in advance. They have taken the liberty of writing out for you. All you have to do is sign the new contract."

"I would get that checked out first, Jo. It seems a bit forward," Allan interrupted.

"Settle down Allan," Steve said. "It's all good, Jo. He doesn't know what he is talking about."

I chatted with Steve for a little while and decided that I would have to negotiate the updated plans with Julie and I will come back tomorrow and sort out what needs doing before we go any further. I also wanted to talk more to Allan about what can be done to save Caplin. I finished my discussion with Steve, and Allan drove me back to the homestead. There was not much Allan could fill me in on about Caplin so I told him I would come into town in the next few days and have a chat with the local Elders' property manager. Back at the house, Allan dropped me off and headed on his way. I went inside and Julie was preparing afternoon tea. I could smell the scones from half a mile away, whilst the pot of tea was brewing. I told Julie of the proposal and she understood that the water was a necessary requirement for sure, and agreed to have a look at it with me tomorrow. We will head back out to see Steve then, after all, it is her land and the forty thousand dollar cheque was an enormous amount in these hard times on the land.

The phone rang. It was Phillip Duncan, the Dalgety's manager. Apparently Allan had caught up with him in at his Blackall office and they had talked about Caplin and how I had an interest in its future. I asked him to get the facts and I may be willing to lease the land, at least that way it will hopefully persuade Dalgety's away from the idea of sending the property to auction. Mentally, it was a big day. After being in the peace and quiet of the ride, I was starting to feel a bit fatigued.

"Enough with business for today," I said. "Let's get the barbecue going for an early dinner."

"Sounds cool!" Jack replied. "I will help get some wood to light the fire."

"I will get the grog," said Dave, as he headed into the bar room.

Time to chill out, for the day is winding down and there's always tomorrow to do what didn't get done today. The word had got around and most of the staff pitched in to help. Such a great night was had by all. The sun went down leaving a long twilight of orange and red.

It was Friday morning, and the week had gone quick. Julie had left early this morning with her friend Rebecca. There was sale at the saddlery outside of Longreach. I waited for Dave and Jack to make their way to the house as they have been discussing moving on. I think the boys have got itchy feet. I started going through the paperwork. The accounts are something I tend to leave for someone else, I guess it's a bad habit I learned over the years, but one I should rectify.

At about nine thirty, Dave and Jack arrived. I had just put the kettle on the stove to boil.

"How are you two going? Can I interest you in a cuppa?" I said.

"Yeah, go ahead. I am up for one," said Jack.

"Me too!" Dave insisted.

Dave had told me about his interest in a property out Charleville way, almost three hundred acres, he claimed. It was a good spread and needed 5 thousand dollars as a deposit. I could see a bit of a con going on here so I continued on a different subject. I needed to change the fences around the water pump site and build a diversion road away from the main gateway, this would mean talking to the neighbour and convince him to allow access into the area.

Meanwhile, the phone rang. It was Phillip Duncan, the guy I spoke to on the phone yesterday. He had sorted out a deal with Caplin Station and asked if I was interested in the property. A lot of financial big words were used mostly. I just listened, even though I didn't have a clue what he was saying. The bottom line was that Dalgety's had refinanced the property to Noat's old man a few years ago and they have regained the deeds to the property.

"If you can come up with seventy thousand dollars, the property is yours. We will cover our losses."

Mmm! My ears pricked up and I knew I had a cheque for forty thousand dollars, but how could I get the other thirty?

"I still have to talk it over with Julie, of course. That would possibly be harder to get her approval than the money," I jokingly replied.

It ended up being a long day. This paperwork caper is starting to get the better of me. Not long after I had coffee with the boys this morning, the local minister had turned up and informed me that Noat was not doing too well being on remand, awaiting his trial.

"Is there any chance you can go see him soon, Jo?" The Reverend asked.

"I will go and see him in a couple of days," I replied.

Noat and I have been family for years, but I didn't know what his intentions were. I phoned the barrister handling his case and he said things were going well and that he had sourced the courts for a negotiation, hoping for an acquittal. It all seems to be coming together. I was convinced that buying Caplin Station and letting Noat manage the place is the best thing I could do to keep his spirits alive, He only ever knew of being there since his birth. I tried to organise the bookwork so it was basic and I could keep track of it. I was very proud of my efforts, but it is bound to be wrong.

The phone rang again, but this time it was Julie on the other end letting me know that she would be staying at her friend's house overnight, and could I come and get her in the morning.

"Yes, that will be okay," I said, putting down the phone.

I heard a vehicle approaching the front of the house. It was Merv. I hadn't seen him for a few months now.

"G'day, mate," I said, as I walked out on the veranda.

"What brings you around here?"

"I just heard the news about Julie," he said. "Very sad."

This puzzled me.

"I just got off the phone to Julie?" I said, questioningly, not having a clue what he was carrying on about.

"That bloody cancer, it's a bastard disease. It doesn't care who it takes."

"WHAT?" I asked. "What stuffing cancer? And who?"

Maureen had spoken to Katie in the pie shop, who heard from Jim the barber, who is married to the Longreach hospital Matron, that Julie has liver cancer.

I dropped to my knees in disbelief. Holding my head in the palms of my hands, the tears seem to flow like a stream. Merv was very apologetic.

"I thought you must have known. So sorry mate. It's about normal word of mouth on these areas. It moves faster than a fire in the summer time."

I was left drained by the news. I could not help myself. I got into the car and headed into Longreach. My mind kept on asking the same question: Why didn't Julie say something?

I raced down the road. I was angry, but astounded that half the town knew about Julie's condition before me.

The dry weather had caused small rocks to scatter across the surface of the road. I was driving way too fast, but my heart was doing the driving not my head. I came into the narrow section over the single lane bridge, and as I approached it, so did the local school bus. I had no choice but turn the wheel and go down the embankment, as I was unable to stop in time.

Well, just my luck. A dirty, big bloody hole where a tree had been removed since the last lot of storms sat in the embankment, and swallowed the front right hand corner of the car. This made the vehicle flip over onto its roof.

Anticipating the car going over, I leant across the seat and gripped onto the underside and hung on for dear life.

My ride finished after another three rolls down the embankment. The car laid against an old ghost gum. I ended up on the back seat amongst the feed buckets. It is not a real good idea to try and hang on with only having one leg. I heard the bus take off again. It must have stopped when I went over the edge. I was sure someone must have got off the bus and hoped they were able to get down to see if I was okay.

I managed to get my head out of the window and started calling so they could hear me. I waited another five minutes and tried again in vain. Eventually I came to the conclusion that no one was out there. I felt trails of blood running down my back from shoulder height to the waist. My left arm was trapped.

I don't know much about what happened after that, as my head felt sore and my eyes heavy. I can only assume a few hours later when regained consciousness, that the car had cooled down. No more steam pouring into my car, which now resembled a cocoon. I listened for a while but there was not a vehicle in the area. It was deadly silent.

I reached out to manoeuvre myself closer to the door, but with my arm stuck, it was pointless. It seemed like hours had passed. I nodded off a few times, and my normally patient nature was turning into a panic stricken fury. I just about tore my arm off in my last panic attack. It did me no favours as now I have probably dislocated my shoulder.

I did not know how long I had been asleep. Was it morning? Or was it night? I am so confused. I just lay waiting. The pain has started to ease, or maybe I have managed to ignore it for a while, hard to say.

The sound of a large vehicle, possibly a truck, echoed from the other side of the bridge. As it got closer I could hear the vehicle slow to a halt. The air dispersed from the brakes. I yelled with all my might, screaming like a rampant bull.

"Hang on, mate. I'm going to come down to help. Just hang on."

I could hear him opening tool boxes on the truck. Shortly after, the sound of a rope hitting the car gave me hope of being rescued by this Good Samaritan. It took a while before he made it down to me. I could see a shadow of a large man. It was Earl, the bloke who owns the piggery.

He weighed close to 29 stone, one hell of a package. I could only think of the two of us now stuck down this friggin' gully.

"Hey! It's you, Jo! Have you got that ten bucks you owe me, you scoundrel?"

Earl chuckled as he attempted to get me free. I have seen this bloke throw full size pigs into the trailer with his bare hands. This his shoulder against the car, he pushed it so the door cleared the ground. Reefing the door ajar, my arm was still caught between the roof and the back of the seat. Holding me firmly, Earl hit against the inner floor panel, slamming it like a jack hammer, an inch at a time, until I fell forward. My arm finally released from the entrapment. Out of the car, I laid with my arm twisted like a pretzel. I brought it across my chest and used my shirt to hold to in place. Looking over at Earl, he was chasing his breath, with a face red like a ripe tomato.

"You okay there, Earl?" I said.

"Fit as a fiddle," Earl replied. "Now, how the bloody hell do we get back to the road? You might have to carry me, Jo!"

About ten minutes past and the big fella had returned to his normal colour. I had my arm supported by tying the sleeve of my shirt round my wrist. The rope was full of knots from where it had broken over the years, which helped me make my way up the steep embankment.

About ten feet from the top, I heard another vehicle coming down the road. It didn't sound like it was going to stop, then all of a sudden, the rope was pulled from my hand with a torrent of force. I managed to get a grip of the weeds and lifted myself to the roadway. Looking at the rope, Earl had tied it from his truck on the other side of the road. No wonder it ripped out of my hand when the car went racing through. Never trust a pig farmer when it comes to safety, I thought to myself.

No chance of me creating another knot in this rope, and with one hand I opened the toolbox, only to be bitten by Earl's red cattle dog, Dippy.

"Get out of it, you mongrel!" I shouted.

Dippy shot off to look for Earl. Three more ropes, shorter than the one Earl had used, lay on the bottom of the box. None of them any good to me. Searching the best I could, another car came along. I waved it down. It was Stuart, my auctioneer friend from Tennant Creek.

"Give us hand, can ya?" I called as he pulled up.

"Crikey, Jo! What happened to you?"

"No time to talk, Stu. We have to get Big Earl up from my wreck."

Well Stuart was all of 9 stone, thin as a stick. A good wind would blow him away.

"I have a long rope in the back. I will get it out and take it down to him."

His lanky legs had a stride of ten feet, I reckon. In no time he was over the side and down to Earl, which would have been better if he had given me one end of the bloody rope. He tied the rope around Earl and struggled back up.

"Sorry, Jo. I was a little bit eager and I forgot to give you the other end," he said with an embarrassing grin.

Stuart's Ute had a winch on the bullbar, so I got him to drive towards the edge and he gave me the cable controls whilst he descended back down to Earl. I waited for his instructions.

"Give it a go, Jo!" He yelled.

The controls had two buttons. I guessed the top one was up, so I triggered it. Oops! That was down.

"Shit!" I heard Stu yell. "Get off me you heifer! Hurry Jo, he is squashing me!"

I only had one choice, the other button. Now it was my turn to be red faced.

The comical of eras would not have been so bad if it wasn't for the pain shooting down my arm. Somehow I think it is not a good look to see a one legged man with his arm in a sling. I held the button raising Earl from the drop. He was about three quarters the way up when I swear the back wheels lifted on the Ute. His heavy weight structure was pushing the equipment to its limits.

Eventually we all got back to the road. It was about then that an ambulance was travelling from Jundah to Longreach. They stopped to see if we needed help. I was feeling weak from my time trapped in the car so I had some water and dry biscuits that they had in the lunch box whilst they treated my arm.

All I could think about in my time down the embankment was seeing Julie. I wasn't that badly knocked about but the ambulance officers offered to take me to Longreach. It took about an hour to get to the hospital. Along the way, I nodded off a few times. I was told that I was concussed and Alfred, one of the ambos, put in a drip in to get my dehydration under control.

The ambulance pulled into the loading bay. I was able to walk but the put me in a wheel chair anyway.

"I need to see Julie," I said to the head nurse.

"Julie Archer?" She replied. "She was released two days ago."

Not knowing what day it was, I shook my head with tears building up in the corners of my eyes.

The nurse said, "I will call her and let her know you are here."

I was put into a supervised room for 24 hours. The nurse came back and told me Julie had been told of me being in hospital and that I was okay.

"I told her you would ring her shortly. It is good news that the cancer scare Julie had turned out to be just an infection in the liver. You must be relieved!" The nurse commented.

"Bloody hell! Last thing I remember was being told of Julie's liver cancer, now it turns out that she has the all clear and I am the one who almost died. Shit! Life can be such a twisted journey some days." I replied.

Once the doctor had finished with me I was allowed to use the phone in the Nurse's station to call Julie. Our conversation really didn't go anywhere. I turned into a river of tears and Julie was so overwhelmed that I was okay that we just could not talk. I have, for the first time in my life, realised what love actually is.

I stayed in hospital under observation for another 32 hours. I was so relieved when Julie walked in the door, it lifted my spirits high. I just could not wait to hold her.

My arm was feeling a lot better and I was still having the occasional dizzy spell, but nothing I cannot deal with.

"Just get me out this place," I pleaded.

The rest of the week was very strange. We both had a lot to say to each other but neither of us touched on our thoughts. I asked Julie to sit on the veranda, and I poured a glass of wine and started to open up about what was bugging me. Gently as I could, I asked why she did not include me in her cancer test. We are supposed to be there for each other, I thought.

"Well Jo, I only found out the day I went into town to look for wedding supplies. I popped in to see the doctor and he had the results of a blood test from the month earlier. His advice was to stay in overnight and do some more tests. I never thought much about it. I was concerned, but not worried. So that's why I told you I was staying at a friend's house. I cannot understand where you got the idea that I had liver cancer though. I bet you it was those gossips at the hospital. So much for patient confidentiality!" Julie exclaimed.

"I heard it from Merv, who heard it from… Oh it's just shambles! I lost it and decided to go into Longreach to see you, when I lost control of the car. Oh, um, by the way, sorry about your BMW."

I stuttered as the lump in my throat grew bigger.

CHAPTER NINE

The focus has now been set on our upcoming wedding. With only ten days left there is a lot to do. Nat, the stable hand, has now come back to work for us. I still don't know whether she has accepted my apologies from when I shunned her riding abilities last time she worked here at Archer Station. But it also turns out that she has outstanding flower arranging skills.

Merv had found some tents which were almost as big as circus tents. I don't know where he got them from and it's probably better not to ask. The little bit of rain we had really changed the appearance of the grounds. The grass looked lush and the flowers were well on the way towards blooming. The conversation of Julie's BMW had come up a few times, and I tried to put it out of context but Merv just kept on saying how badly destroyed it was. I had, only a few days earlier, found out that the car was the last thing Julie's father had bought for her before the family's tragic departure. So it was a sensitive subject.

The workers on the water project have offered to help with the wedding preparations, which is a great help. They had levelled out an area about fifty feet from the house and were building an outdoor dance platform, and on the other side they have delivered sand to make a horse arena. You cannot have a wedding in the outback without some barrel racing.

It was all coming together. I felt that Julie had brought a positive attitude to the upcoming celebration of marriage. Normally nothing gets done until the last moment but this time we are sticking to the plan.

I heard the telephone ring. Shit! I had completely forgotten about my negotiations with Dalgety's over Caplin Station. Their offer is still on the table which is great, considering I had told them I was unable to continue with negotiations right now as the timing was too close to Julie and I getting married. They were happy to put it on hold until I can get back to them.

The insurance assessor arrived with an offer for payment covering Julie's car. I left Julie to discuss the finer points and went down to the stables to check the horses. Dave and Jack were there.

"You were bloody lucky, Jo!" Jack shouted.

As I got closer, Dave just winked as an indication he was glad I was safe. Upon closer inspection, I noticed something behind Dave. I couldn't believe my eyes! Dave was standing in front of Baily Jo, my horse from Caplin.

"How did you get hold of him?" I questioned Dave.

"Well Adam Swartz, the meat bloke, seen him and recognised our brand. So Jack and I went and got him. He is a bit thin, but won't take long to bring him back up to scratch."

It was good to see Baily Jo. I know I am unable to ride him again, but he is a good boy and deserves the best. Julie had followed me down to the stables. I was taken by surprise when I looked around and seen her and Nat standing behind me. A moment with a lot of care and heartfelt content was shared by all.

The next week was very tense. The socialising aspects of getting married in the country definitely is a town affair.

I think I have met every elderly lady from the YWCA and the auxiliary group from around the area. I have never worked so hard. Every time I try to have a beer, someone would interrupt and back to work I would go. I will be glad when it's over, I thought to myself.

Archer Station was looking excellent. The gazebo that Tony and Neville had built was sitting pride and place in the centre of the yard. The girls were getting all clucky and talking about babies.

"Now hang on a minute!" I said. "First things first, huh?"

I decided to lay low for a while down at the stables. I sat talking to my old horse, Bailey Jo. He doesn't get ridden much now days. He is more of a yard horse, but most likely the best guard dog you will ever meet.

The sun was on its way down and I had been chatting away to Bailey Jo for hours without realising I had an audience. Nat, Jack and Dave had been standing near the stables listening to the stories I told to my horse.

"Geez, Jo! I never knew you had such a talent for talking. You normally say bugger all to us." Jack chuckled with that shonky grin of his.

"You will get yours, you skinny black bugger! Just remember who's paying your wages." I commented.

Heading back to the house, Nat took the old tractor up to move some debris from the storm we had a couple of days ago. Merv had arrived with Stuart, and Earl was following close behind. It was good to see the other two. We haven't seen each other since my accident.

As we thought we had plenty of time, it dawned on us there were only twenty four hours until wedding. Tony, Jack, Dave, Merv and Earl were busy having pre-wedding drinks, although they were pretending to be working. Even a blind teddy could see what they were up to.

Julie has a lot of her friends over for the evening hoping to get everything thing finalised before the ten o'clock ceremony.

Oh what the heck, I thought as I reached for a beer and sat down with the boys for a farewell drink. No more freedom once Julie gets the ownership papers. I will be stuffed, as Merv would say.

The sun was going down and I was banned from entering the house, so I just sat outside and talked out loud to make my presence known. Jack had parked his Ute beside the fence with the radio so loud the windscreen wipers were bouncing across the glass.

The twilight was shimmering across the spread. The lights of a vehicle entered the long driveway. Slowly it came into view. It was a police car. What have we done now? I thought to myself. Jack and Dave both took off like turkeys in the scrub as the vehicle pulled up. A male figure wearing a suit descended from the passenger side. It is never any good when the law comes wearing a tie.

"What the bloody hell are you up to, Jo?" Noat's voice echoed across the deck.

"Well, I'll be buggered! How did you bribe your way out, Noat?" I chuckled and went to greet him.

"They let me out. The jury said there was not enough evidence to sentence me, so reasonable doubt had given me freedom. Besides, I heard there was a party going on.

Young Johnno, Earl's son, brought me out to join in.

Well, where is my beer? That's the least you can do for me!" Noat commented.

Jack and Dave returned, inch by inch, until they recognised Noat. Then it was on like a big free for all. They were all over him.

It didn't seem that long but with all the talking, drinking and obnoxious behaviour, the morning light was appearing on the horizon. Only five more hours until I tie the knot. My nerves were starting to kick in. Oh, what the heck! Another beer won't hurt.

At around 8:30 Jack woke up and gave me kick in the guts.

"Come on, get up! You have to start getting ready. Julie is going to kill me if you don't look your best."

And with that, Merv walked up, grabbed me, and through me over his shoulder. Merrily, we clambered over to the horse trough, and threw me in. Well, I don't know if it was the water bringing me around, or the smell of the two dead birds in the unused old bath, but I shot up and shook like a dirty old dog. I tried to get stable on my feet, it took a few attempts but eventually I got there.

Rebecca came out of the house in a panic, "What's all the carry on?" She said. "Why aren't you starting to get ready? Get around to the worker's cottage and try to sort yourself out, or I will give you a fat lip, right?"

I had a shower and walked out to see Jack wearing Merv's trousers. He was standing in one leg hole.

"Somehow I don't think these are my dacks," he laughed as Merv took one look at the ones he had.

"I ain't even going to try putting these on." Merv said, shaking Jack's pants about.

Nine thirty arrived sooner than the cattle at feed time. We made our way around to the pergola area and stood in our position which we had practiced during the wedding rehearsal. It was a beautiful day. The sun was out and the sounds of violins were ascending from within the house. The sound of live music brought a realisation of how much I was looking forward to taking Julie as my wife, my partner, my soulmate for good.

"It's time!" Dave yelled as everyone had arrived. Most had to stand as the whole township had come to see this memorable moment when the girl that Blackall loved so much was to wed the love of her life. Okay, well, I put in the love of her life in. I gotta have some credit, don't I?

The big ten foot high doors at the entry to the house opened slowly with the two flower girls in sight. My knees trembled and the night of drinking was pouring out of me in a river of sweat. The girls walked forward into the sight of the guests. They looked beautiful. Karen and Trina, the first two bridesmaids, stepped out. Not far behind, wearing gowns that would make royalty jealous, Nat and Rebecca came out next. Wow! I started to feel pale. The heat of the morning and the excitement in anticipating seeing Julie walk out the door was getting to me. The flower girls and bridesmaids made their way down, lining up down the porch steps. Everyone turned to view my lovely bride that appeared from within the house. The violins that Rebecca's friends were playing made the atmosphere seem like a scene out of a Ginger Rogers' movie. I was gobsmacked. My tongue was unable to get back into my mouth.

Wow!

One step at a time, almost like slow motion, Julie came into the light, and standing beside her was none other than Noat, who Julie had asked to give her away earlier on today. That sneaky dog! Never let on about his duties for this morning. The girls had thrown rose petals across the porch which almost looked like rubies glistening in the sunlight. As Julie approached the row of chairs each side of the makeshift aisle, I noticed that she was wearing western boots. Her dress was magnificent, but why the boots? I thought. Never the less, I watched every movement that her shapely body took.

Noat walked Julie up beside me and proceeded to sit down. I looked directly into Julie's eyes through the veil. I could see her mesmerising eyes beaming back at me.

Rebecca lifted the veil to show Julie's now watery eyes. Her lips were trembling. This is a big moment for her with no family to see this beautiful day. I touched her on the cheek and whispered thank you as I held her hand.

This was not a really good idea, as when a chick is stressed, you can imagine, I almost lost circulation to my fingers. The ceremony was very short and sweet and although the vows were basic, we added words of our own which included,

"Go forth as one with two hearts today and forever. Like birds of a feather, the wind beneath our sails."

These were words that had been carved into her father's chair in the living room. Apparently he wrote these words when he married Julie's mother. Neither of us knew what they meant, but it was some comfort to Julie to read them out on our special day.

Now comes the best part where I get to kiss the bride. I wrapped my arms around her like a python. I pressed my body against hers, losing my balance. The sweat had run down my back and under my stump which made my false leg give out, and as usual, ass up I went, taking Julie with me. Too bad if we were hurt, as everyone was laughing so hard you couldn't hear the music.

Well country living has its advantages. The feast was about to begin, Jack had organised the music so we were in for treat. Heading out of the gazebo after the signing was done, John Denver's 'Thank God I'm A Country Boy' started playing. All of a sudden, the wedding went from civilised mode to a country throw down, yee ha!

Whilst Julie and I followed the photographer around, the others prepared the seating and organised the guests in the appropriate locations. Julie took the boots off and wore tall stiletto style shoes. I asked her why the boots and she told me they were her mother's. I just didn't know what to say.

Well it's time to honour all our guests and start the festivities. Merv was in charge of the bar, which was flowing faster than the Thompson River at Longreach.

Jack and Dave, along with Noat, were hanging around the bridal table trying to get me to lash out at them, but I remained civilised, at least for the moment. Duncan Taite was the MC for the night. He was Julie's brother's best friend who had known the family since his early childhood and I had become good friends with him. But honestly, he only got to do it because Noat was expected to still be in the lockup.

The speeches got under way, and I tell you what, some of them were very good. The others, I think the jury is still out. The late afternoon turned into evening. The backup supply of grog had just arrived. Merv's old dodge postal truck definitely came in handy today. Well, I was waiting for the party to thin out but by ten o'clock I think there were more people here now than when we first started. Oh well! The Australian outback spirit strives as mate ship overcomes bad times.

Merv was having trouble breathing and left the area. He didn't say anything just went around the corner, where he fell to the ground. The rest of us just continued enjoying ourselves, none the wiser of Merv's demise.

I sat on the front porch with Julie. We talked about how happy we both were to find true love when so many others are still waiting. The moon was full, the clouds had moved on and Archer Station was under a big spot of moonlight. The beauty of romance still blossoming between myself and Julie. I started to talk about the future. Julie stopped me in my tracks with these softly spoken words:

"Eight months and ten days to go."

I looked at her, puzzled. Then it hit me. We were, or Julie

was, I don't know! A baby is on the way! I jumped for joy, whilst Julie told me to be quiet as no one needs to know yet.

"Please honey, just keep it to yourself and come here," she said.

I was so excited. I went to sit next to her, when out of the corner of my eye, Merv was slumped beside the house. My life has just started a new chapter, but Merv was about to finish his.

THE END

RINGER OF DUSTY PLAINS